Romans 16:7

ασπασασθε ανδρονικον και **ιουνιαν** τουσ συγγενεισ μου και συναιχμαλωτουσ μου οιτινεσ εισιν **επισημοι εν τοισ αποστολοισ** οι και προ εμου γεγονασιν εν χριστω

To contact the author send emails to:

david@djbournemouth.co.uk

Acknowledgments

This book originated in the autumn of 2013 in a series of Bible studies on the issue of women in the church, in which the subject of Junia was covered by me over three studies. The spoken word in conjunction with PowerPoint could only convey the message up to a point, and thus the seeds were sown to reduce the message to writing.

Not everyone agreed with my point of view and some refused to accept there was a woman apostle. For various reasons some of those who disagreed were either unable or unwilling to attend the studies. Prior to giving them, I confirmed I was willing to make audio recordings of the studies available, together with the PowerPoint presentation and my speaking notes. This was accompanied with an offer that if they were still unconvinced by my arguments I would meet with them at a time of their choosing to debate the matter further.

This book is my way of keeping to my side of the bargain.

JUNIA

A WOMAN

AN APOSTLE

David Williams

To Mum

If only those who say a woman cannot teach or preach
could teach or preach as well as you.

Contents

Preface

For some time I have been concerned at the number of Christians I come across who appear unable to give an explanation for things that they do, say or believe. Whilst it would be unfair to require every Christian to be an expert theologian, it strikes me as eminently desirable that they be able to give cogent reasons for their beliefs, at a level that is commensurate with their intellectual ability and understanding.

When it comes to the issue of 'women in the church' (by which I mean the debate as to whether Scripture teaches there are any roles or functions in the church which are not open to women), I readily acknowledge that for many years I accepted a situation or tacitly believed in something for which I could give no sensible explanation. I could not explain why, from Scripture, I believed it was okay for a woman to preach, or to be an elder or a deacon.

Having been awakened to this failing I endeavoured to study the subject to the best of my ability. In doing so my knowledge of the arguments on both sides of the debate obviously increased and having considered those arguments I remain of the same view about women in the church as I did before, only now I feel able to justify it. However, after spending many hours pouring over books and articles and listening to various talks and lectures, it struck me that the authors and speakers invariably assume a level of knowledge that is beyond that of the average 'person in the pew'. The most obvious and frustrating example would be when a passage appears in Greek or Latin with no English translation, the reader being assumed to be fluent in one or both!

The result was that I found myself spending a great deal of time 'getting up to speed'. Books on 'New Testament Greek' had to be purchased and read, not to mention working out how to install and use a Greek font on an English computer/keyboard!

The issue of 'women in the church' is a big one. It involves looking at many words, verses and passages in both the Old and New Testament. Countless books and articles have been written in support of various views, which rather begs the question of why write another one? My answer is that I am trying to approach the issue in a slightly different way. On the one hand I want to write a book that is thorough and deals with the relevant arguments, whilst on the other I want it to be a book for the 'person in the pew'. In other words, easy to understand and requiring no technical or linguistic expertise on the part of the reader. It is a difficult balancing act but one which I hope I have just about managed.

The subject is too big to deal with in one go. For that reason this book deals with just one limited question – was there a female apostle? Even on this limited question it is impossible to do justice to all the relevant arguments without descending into detail and some technical points. In particular, dealing with New Testament Greek cannot be avoided. Having experienced at first hand the frustration and annoyance of reading a book where the author assumes the reader to have a level of knowledge of New Testament Greek which far exceeds mine, I have done everything I can to avoid doing likewise. For that reason the sections on Greek may be teaching some how to suck the proverbial egg, but for others they will hopefully be informative and easy to understand.

I do not claim to be presenting new arguments. Indeed, I wish to place on record that little, if any, of the material in this book is my own. My role has simply been to draw material from various sources and try to present one, easy to understand, coherent argument as to why I am convinced the Bible speaks of a female apostle. For ease of reading I have avoided the use of footnotes, but the sources from which virtually all my material has been drawn are listed in the bibliography at the back of the book. For those who wish to explore the subject in more detail I would highly recommend the items on that list. As for the explanations and tables on New Testament Greek, these have been adapted from the book by William Mounce called 'Basics of Biblical Greek', which I would highly recommend to anyone who wants to learn New Testament Greek.

Finally, I would like to thank friends and family for taking the time to proof read my drafts and for their suggested amendments. They have certainly greatly reduced the error count in the text, but for those that remain I take full and sole responsibility.

CHAPTER 1

The Background

The general questions on the issue of 'women in the Church' often take the form of; can a woman preach, teach, sing, prophesy, pray, lead worship? That's not an exhaustive list, other points can be added and there are some nuances. For example, even if a woman can teach, can she do so just to other women or children, or can she teach men as well?

Intrinsically linked to that list of questions are those questions that ask; can a woman be a deacon, an elder, a pastor or an apostle?

People can hold very strong and passionate views on these questions. In fact, such has been my experience that I think it essential to draw attention to a quote, which ought to be considered and accepted by all.

> "We must recognize that those who hold different views than ours may be just as honest, well-intentioned and well-informed interpreters of Scripture as we think we are or try to be. There is nothing wrong with sharing our views, trying to convince others of our position, or pointing out weaknesses in other people's views, but we must keep in mind that our salvation and Christian witness to others is not ultimately determined by the position we take on this complex issue."

Unfortunately, history shows that not everyone is willing or able to adopt this approach. There are extremes on both sides and that's unfortunate. For my part I simply want to set out my view and the basis for my holding it. If you agree with it, fine. If you don't, equally fine. We should be able to discuss, examine, test and evaluate our points of view and should be able and willing, if necessary, to agree to differ.

Guiding Principles

Before getting into the arguments it is important to establish the rules of the game, or what might better be described as guiding principles. They may not be universally accepted, they are certainly not an exhaustive list, but they do form the foundation for what follows and they deserve careful consideration.

Bias.

I am biased. I can say that quite comfortably and quite honestly. I might also add that so is everyone else. Every single person who comes to this debate will have a preconceived idea or view. They will already have a position or a leaning, and that is a bias. It does not follow that this is in some way wrong. There is nothing wrong with bias in certain situations and nothing wrong with having a preconceived view or leaning on this or any other subject.

What is important about bias is that people are upfront about it, recognize it and appreciate it can affect their view or cloud their judgment. It can affect what I'm going to say, it can affect what I'm going to believe. It might mean that I look at one argument less critically than another. However, the more honest and aware we are about it, the more chance there is of us not allowing it to prevent us finding the truth.

Scholarship

In a strange way the definition of scholarship can be quite subjective, so to avoid misunderstanding it is important to clarify what I mean. In short, I am taking it to mean the gold standard of academia, a kind of quality assurance mark, which we should all try to achieve. One example of how this applies in practice is the need to recognise that there are arguments on both sides and ensuring that you are familiar with those arguments, not just the one(s) you agree with. It demands familiarity with an argument be obtained by reading or studying that argument, as opposed to someone else's interpretation or critique of it.

There are plenty of books that deal with the issue of women in the Church. For example, Wayne Grudem has written a book called 'Evangelical Feminism and Biblical Truth'. Including the index and appendices it runs to over 800 pages. In this book he outlines other people's arguments and says why they are wrong. My definition of scholarship prevents you from simply taking his word for it. It demands that you familiarise yourself with those arguments first hand, not through Grudem's lens. I am not saying you can't agree with his conclusions, just that scholarship demands more than a blind acceptance of whatever he, or anyone else says.

If it's not obvious to you already, as you read this book you will realise I disagree with Wayne Grudem. Not on everything, but on certain things and very much so in respect of Junia. I disagree with him not because I have read other people who have said why they disagree with him, I disagree with him because I've read his argument, examined it and found it wanting.

Experts

That takes me to experts. In the context of the local Church we tend to view the pastor or leader as the expert. In college life it is the professor. But experts do not and must not be allowed to decide arguments. You cannot decide whether something is right or wrong simply because an expert says it is right or wrong. Evidence decides arguments, not experts.

A legal analogy may assist. If you were on a jury and you had an expert in front of you (in any field, it could be medical, ballistics, forensic), that expert will give an opinion. But he or she doesn't get to decide the case, doesn't get to decide the argument. You do. That's because you are members of the jury. The expert can present his/her opinion and, importantly, can say why they hold that opinion. If you happen to believe that the reasons for the opinion are valid, then you are going to agree with it. If you don't, you can disagree with it (provided you have good grounds for doing so), and the decision is yours, because you are making the decision, not the expert.

A man called Robert Dick Wilson perhaps best explained this point. He lived in the late 1800's/early 1900's and was a phenomenal intellectual. Depending on whom you read, he was fluent in 40 to 50 languages. He was fluent in every single language that the Old Testament had ever been written in. He was also fluent in all the languages of the people that lived around the time of the Old Testament. He spoke dialects of ancient languages such as Babylonian and Hittite. He travelled the world and dedicated his life to study and at the end of it he was widely regarded as one of, if not the most authoritative experts on the Old Testament and its original manuscripts.

He said this about experts:

> *"If a man is called an expert, the first thing to be done is to establish the fact that he is such; one expert may be worth more than a million other witnesses that are not experts. You will have observed that the critics of the Bible who go to it in order to find fault have a most singular way of claiming to themselves all knowledge and all virtue and all love of truth. One of their favourite phrases is, 'All scholars agree'. I wish to know who the scholars are and why they agree. Where do they get their evidence from to start with? My point is that you ought to be able to trace back this agreement amongst scholars to the original scholar who propounded the statement and then find out whether what that scholar said is true. What was the foundation of his statement?"*

In other words, the foundation; what was the evidence that led him or her to make the statement that they did?

Evidence

In respect of evidence, you have got to ask yourself, is it evidence and is it the best evidence? If it's not the best evidence, can we get better evidence, and if it's not evidence then why should it be taken into account?

Evidence will always trump opinion, including expert opinion. An expert's opinion is valuable, but identifying the basis for that opinion is of much greater value.

Thus, as we examine the question of whether the Bible speaks of a female apostle, the principles of bias, scholarship, experts and evidence must be kept at the forefront of our minds.

CHAPTER 2

Definitions

It is easy to assume people are familiar with words and terminology when it isn't necessarily the case. Anyone who dips their toe into the water that is the subject of women in the Church will almost immediately hear words such as 'complementarian', 'hierarchists', 'egalitarian', and 'feminists' being bandied about. Given a little more time they may observe that such words are often used more as an insult than a description of what someone is or believes. To continue the water analogy, if you want to give the impression of being fully immersed in the 'women in the Church' debate, you should know that the good insults are 'feminist' or 'liberal' on the one side and 'authoritarian' or 'male chauvinist' on the other.

It is not my intention to give long definitions of each word. For the purposes of this book, however, I'm going to use the terms, "Complementarian" and "Egalitarian", so it is only right that I explain what I take those two words to mean.

An Egalitarian will say that there is equality between men and women. This needs to be clarified because a Complementarian will say that as well. For an Egalitarian, equality between men and women means that when it comes to roles in the Church they would be open to either. There are different views within the Egalitarian camp, but that is a general definition of an Egalitarian.

A Complementarian will also say there is equality between men and women, but, as the word 'Complementarian' suggests, men and women complement each other, and they do so by performing different roles and functions. Thus, equality between men and women does not mean to say that they can or should carry out the same roles or functions. This applies to roles and functions in the Church, which a Complementarian would say are only open to men, not women.

I might add that whilst for convenience sake I am defining these terms, this should not be taken to mean I agree with the positions advanced by those definitions. In particular, I do not accept as a matter of logic that Person A (woman) can be said to be equal with Person B (man) if at the same time Person A is being prohibited from performing a role that Person B can perform solely because Person A is a woman. The crucial factor is that the prohibition is not based on ability, qualification or gifting (which as a basis of prohibition would not violate the concept of equality), but rather it is based on the nature, the very essence of the person. To see my point try substituting the words 'black man' and 'white man' for the words in brackets in respect of Person A and Person B. Exactly how equal does a Complementarian think a black man would feel if he was told he couldn't do a job a white man could do solely because he was black?

And a short word on debating

When it comes to debate, people are different. Some people like to discuss things calmly, others less so. I have experience of both. I'm very keen to discuss things calmly, but recognise that it doesn't take much to encourage me to discuss things the other way! The simple fact is that 'women in the Church' is a controversial subject and emotions can run high. In addition, it is unfortunate that some people go too far and arguments are made which are nonsense and silly.

For example, I have no time for the argument which asserts that someone who holds the Complementarian view is supporting and/or supports male domination or abuse of women, or that their view leads to domestic violence. I have no time for that because I don't think that's what a genuine Complementarian believes and I think it's a distortion of their view.

Equally, there are some on the Complementarian side who argue that anyone who holds an Egalitarian view is a biblical liberal who will accept anything, doesn't accept the word of God and will end up accepting any number of unbiblical teachings. Put another way,

Egalitarianism is the start of some kind of slippery slope that inevitably and inexorably leads to liberalism and error. I have no time for that argument either. It simply doesn't add up, the evidence doesn't support it and it does not follow as a matter of logic.

CHAPTER 3

Why Junia?

As I explained in the preface, this book deals only with the question of whether there was a female apostle. It could have dealt with women elders or deacons or various other issues, so the question naturally arises, why this one?

In 1 Corinthians 12:28 we read *'first apostles, secondarily prophets, thirdly teachers.'* In 1 Corinthians 12:29 we read *'are all apostles are all prophets are all teachers'.* In Ephesians 4:11 we read, *'and he gave some apostles and some prophets and some evangelists and some pastors and teachers.'*

In all those lists the offices or roles are given in an order. Apostles are mentioned first, prophets are mentioned second, teachers are mentioned third. It is commonly considered and accepted that that order represents an order of hierarchy or seniority. In other words, the lists show that an apostle is a higher or more senior position than a prophet and likewise a prophet is more senior than a teacher.

Based on that consideration, some argue that if a woman can prophesy (it being clear from the New Testament that Paul allowed this), then as prophecy is above teaching in the lists it would make sense that a woman can also teach. If you like, if prophecy is job number two in order of seniority, then clearly whoever can do job number two can also do job number three – teacher.

The counter to that argument is that teaching is not the same as prophesying, because unlike prophesying, teaching, or at least certain kinds of teaching, involves an exercise of authority, whereas, it is said, prophesying does not. Therefore, although you might say it comes below prophesying in order of seniority, teaching involves something which prophesying does not. If a woman is not allowed to exercise authority over men (1 Timothy 2:12), then she can prophesy but she can't teach authoritatively.

Thus, it is argued, you cannot use the hierarchical order of prophets over teachers as being some sort of winning argument from Scripture to say a woman can teach.

However, there is a second, related argument that is not so easily dismissed. It is based on a woman being an apostle as opposed to being able to prophesy. The same point is made about an apostle being a more senior position than a teacher, or pastor, but this time the objection that an apostle does not have to exercise authority cannot be made. Because just as a teacher has to exercise authority, everyone, and I mean everyone wherever they are on the spectrum of this argument, accepts that an apostle, being an apostle, requires and involves being able to teach and to exercise authority.

So now, it's not so much the fact that because an apostle is job number one, therefore whoever can do job number one, can do jobs number two, three, four, five etc. Rather the argument is that a woman cannot do job number three (teach) because a woman cannot teach or exercise authority. However, if a woman can do job number one, and if that involves teaching and exercising authority, then it follows that a woman can teach and exercise authority. Thus, a woman cannot be excluded from the position of teacher on the grounds that she cannot teach and exercise authority.

That is why the question of a woman apostle is so hotly contested. No one really hotly contests the prophesying question, but the apostle question is a different matter.

So the question naturally arises, what if the Bible speaks of a female apostle? It would mean, by definition, that at the time of the New Testament Church, there was a female apostle; it would mean that that female apostle could teach, because that's part of the function of being an apostle. And it would mean that that female apostle could exercise authority over men, because that too is part of the function of being an apostle. It immediately becomes apparent why this is a relevant issue. If you allow a woman apostle, you are opening the door (I'm not saying you are conclusively winning the argument) to a wider argument. If at a certain point in time it was okay for a woman to be an apostle, it might be okay for a woman to teach or exercise authority over men.

That is why people argue so much about Junia, a woman apostle who is only mentioned once in the whole Bible. In fact I wonder if it would be possible to find an example of a person in the Bible who is only ever mentioned once who has been argued about more than, or even as much as, Junia.

At this stage it would be remiss of me not to deal with the elephant in the room. Complementarians will not hesitate to point out that as interesting as the arguments about Junia might be, the simple fact is that elsewhere in Scripture the apostle Paul makes it abundantly clear that women cannot teach or exercise authority over a man (1 Tim 2:12). Scripture does not contradict Scripture, so the Complementarian position is that Junia cannot have been a female apostle, as to say otherwise would be contradicting what Paul wrote to Timothy in 1 Tim 2:12.

In later chapters I will deal with the arguments Complementarians put forward when they try to show that Junia was not a female apostle. The point I want to make now, however, is that the apparent contradiction between 1 Tim 2:12 and Junia being a female apostle presents people with a simple choice, assuming that is that they accept the premise that Scripture does not contradict Scripture. That choice is between accepting that Junia was not a female apostle or rejecting the Complementarian interpretation of 1 Tim 2:12.

This book does not deal with the arguments about how 1 Tim 2:12 is to be interpreted. I accept that Scripture does not contradict Scripture and I believe the case for Junia being a female apostle to be unanswerable. As a matter of logical necessity it therefore follows that I do not accept the Complementarian interpretation of 1 Tim 2:12. Exactly the same logical necessity applies to

Complementarians. Given their interpretation of 1 Tim 2:12 they have no choice but to refuse to accept Junia was a female apostle.

On this question of apparent conflict between a female apostle and 1 Tim 2:12 I believe there is a significant difference between my position and that of Complementarians. I reject the Complementarian interpretation of 1 Tim 2:12 on grounds other than because Junia was a female apostle. In other words, my interpretation of 1 Tim 2:12 is not dependant on Junia being a female apostle. The reverse cannot be said of Complementarians. Their interpretation of 1 Tim 2:12 cannot sit side by side with Junia being a female apostle and what I want to draw attention to is how they respond to this apparent conflict. Rather than causing them to question or re-examine their interpretation of 1 Tim 2:12, they simply reject the assertion that Junia was a female apostle.

That is why this book deals with the question of whether Junia was a female apostle. When the question is answered in the affirmative, it strikes at the very heart of the Complementarian position – their interpretation of 1 Tim 2:12.

CHAPTER 4

Romans 16:7

So, does the Bible speak of a female apostle? If you open your Bible at the book of Romans, chapter 16 and verse 7, and if like mine your Bible is the King James Version, you will read the following:

> *"Salute Andronicus and Junia, my kinsmen and my fellow prisoners who are of note among the apostles who also were in Christ before me."*

If your Bible of choice is the English Standard Version (ESV), however, you will read:

> *"Greet Andronicus and Junia, my kinsmen and my fellow prisoners, they are well-known to the apostles and they were in Christ before me."*

Now immediately we see a significant difference between the translations. In the KJV, whoever Andronicus and Junia are, they are *'of note among the apostles,'* but in the ESV they are *'well known to the apostles'*. Put another way, in the KJV Andronicus and Junia were apostles (among the apostles), but in the ESV they were not apostles, just *'well known to the apostles'*.

If you read further on in the ESV, and we'll consider the significance of this shortly, there are two footnotes; one is that Junia could also be read Junias (i.e. Junia with an 's' on the end); the second is that instead of the word 'apostles', it could be translated 'messengers'.

As it happens, the difference between Junia and Junias is highly significant, but before looking at why, it is an interesting exercise to look at how other English Bible translations deal with this verse, specifically in respect of Junia or Junias.

If you had the time and were of a sufficiently boring nature to want to do it, you could go through every single English Bible translation and prepare a list of which ones had 'Junia' and which had 'Junias'. That list would start with Tyndale and continue with Cranmer, Great Bible, Geneva Bible, Bishops, King James, Weymouth, and so on. And all of those would have Junia in the verse. If you then continued in your task, you would come up with a list of Bibles that had Junias. It would contain the Dickinson Bible, Revised Version, Muffet, RSV, Philips, Amplified, New English Bible.

Interestingly, both your lists would contain the New International Version (NIV), an oddity explained by the fact that when the NIV first came out it put Junias in the verse, but in later editions changed this to Junia.

The wonders of modern technology do in fact allow these lists to be compiled in a somewhat less boring manner than might be expected. Applying the principle of scholarship and thus not just taking my word for it, the lists can be compiled by going to www.biblegateway.com. Just enter Romans 16:7 in the search box and then pick a translation from the drop down menu. Although not an option to begin with, once the first translation has been selected and shown, there is an option below the text to show the verse in all English translations.

Having established the various different translations, we can draw them together to see that they provide for eight competing possible explanations or translations for Junia.

1. Junia who was an apostle;
2. Junia who was a messenger;
3. Junia who was known to the apostles;
4. Junia who was known to the messengers;
5. Junias who was an apostle;
6. Junias who was a messenger;
7. Junias who was known to the apostles;
8. Junias who was known to the messengers.

As a result of these eights possible explanations, three important questions arise.

1. Was the person mentioned called Junia or Junias?
2. Were the people referred to apostles or messengers?
3. Was Junia(s) among the group (apostles/messengers) or was Junia(s) known to the group?

Although it may not be immediately apparent as to why, the fact is that the answers to these three questions will give us the answer to the overriding question of whether or not there was a female apostle. Accordingly, the remainder of this book is split into three sections, dealing with each of these questions in turn.

As alluded to above, whether it is Junia or Junias is highly significant and the arguments for and against each are dealt with in subsequent chapters. Suffice it to say, all parties to the debate are agreed that Junia (without the 's') is a woman's name. Thus, the first of the three questions (was the person mentioned called Junia or Junias?) is really the same as asking, was the person a man or a woman?

CHAPTER 5

Man or Woman?

The question arises as to why some Bibles say Junia and others
Junias, and surely we should be able to ascertain beyond any
reasonable doubt whether someone was a man or a woman. My
response would be to draw attention to the following quotation:

> *"We may wish that the Holy Spirit had given us the
> word of God in a language that we could more easily
> understand. But in His mysterious wisdom, He gave it
> to us in Hebrew and in Greek. Hence if we want to
> know the Scriptures, to the study of Greek and Hebrew
> we must go." (J. Gresham Machen, September 25,
> 1929)*

And thus begins the descent into the mystery that is New
Testament Greek!

Please do not be put off by the thought of having to get to grips
with a strange unknown language. There is no suggestion that you
have to become fluent or study it for hours on end. What follows
is very much a beginner's guide to some basic Greek grammar,
which will hopefully be interesting and informative on a general
level, as well as helpful to understanding the specific issues
relating to Junia.

Please also bear in mind that the relevance of some of the Greek
grammar explained below will not necessarily become apparent
until you get to the later chapters which deal with the third
question as to whether Junia was 'among' or 'known to' the
apostles.

As a starting point, this is what Romans 16:7 looks like when it is
written in New Testament Greek. And don't panic, you are not
expected and neither do you need to understand any of it!

Romans 16:7

ασπασασθε ανδρονικον και ιουνιαν τουσ συγγενεισ
μου και συναιχμαλωτουσ μου οιτινεσ εισιν επισημοι εν
τοισ αποστολοισ οι και προ εμου γεγονασιν εν χριστω

Here it is again, but this time with two parts underlined. The first section underlined is one word. It reads 'ιουνιαν'. That is the Greek word which is translated into English as Junia(s).

Romans 16:7

ασπασασθε ανδρονικον και **ιουνιαν** τουσ συγγενεισ
μου και συναιχμαλωτουσ μου οιτινεσ εισιν **επισημοι**
εν τοισ αποστολοισ οι και προ εμου γεγονασιν εν
χριστω

Some of the letters of the Greek alphabet are the same, or at least look the same as English letters. However, they are not identical. By way of illustration, you can see what looks like an English 'v' in the Greek word for Junia. This in fact equates to an English 'n', hence the 'v' in the Greek word for Junia is the 'n' in the English word 'Junia'

The second underlined section is the Greek phrase which either means, 'of note among the apostles', or 'known to the apostles'. That is the phrase which is dealt with in chapters 13-23. So for present purposes all we are looking at is the first underlined word - Junia.

Having wet the appetite for New Testament Greek, we need to get our teeth into it a bit more. The starting point, however, is English grammar.

In English we have what are known as different cases, so for example a word can be either the object of the sentence or the subject of the sentence. If it is the object, it is in the objective case, if the subject, the subjective case. So if I say, 'I kicked the ball', the ball is the object and I am the subject. However, in English you can't tell just from looking at the word 'ball' or 'I' whether they are the object or the subject in a sentence. Instead we have to look at the whole sentence and work out its structure, and in English it's normally the order of the words which determines or helps determine which word is the subject and which the object.

In Greek, unlike with English, you tell the case by the word ending, i.e. the letters on the end of the word. So the letter or letters on the end of the Greek word tell you whether that word is the object or the subject of the sentence (as well as various other cases which we don't need to go into). To complete this bit of the jigsaw you just need to know that the case for the object in Greek is called the Accusative case, and the case for the subject is called the Nominative case.

Thus, the word 'I' in 'I kicked the ball' would be the subject, so in Greek would be written in the Nominative case. The word 'ball' would be the object, so in Greek would be written in the Accusative case.

Please also note, we are only dealing with words that are Nouns.

Don't worry if this is starting to get a bit confusing. All you have to remember and understand is that the ending of a Greek word tells you what case it is, i.e. whether it is the subject or object of the sentence.

It may help to look at Greek words as though they have two parts. The first part, what might be called the root, is the bit that stays the same regardless of what case the word is written in. In other words it's the bit to which the second part of the word is added. The second part is what changes depending on what case the word is being written in.

All should become clear when we look at some actual Greek words (nouns).

Starting with the second part of Greek words, here's a table (followed by an explanation) which sets out what those second parts are, depending on what case the word is written in.

Case Endings

Declension	2	1	2
Nominative singular	ς	-	ν
Genitive singular	υ	ς	υ
Dative singular	ι	ι	ι
Accusative singular	ν	ν	ν
Nominative plural	ι	ι	<u>α</u>
Genitive plural	ων	ων	ων
Dative plural	ις	ις	ις
Accusative plural	υς	ς	<u>α</u>

The 'second parts' of the word are known as case endings. There are 4 'cases' in the table, each appears once in the singular and once in the plural. You do not need to worry about what 'declension' means, simply that this table shows endings for words in the first declension (1) and for words in the second declension (2). Some Greek words (nouns) are in the first declension and others in the second declension.

You can see from the table that if you have a Greek word (noun) in the first declension (middle column) which is in the singular and which is the Object (Accusative) of the sentence, it will end (its second part) with the letter 'ν'. If that same word were in the plural, however, it would end with the letter 'ς'

The next table develops the ending of the word a bit further by showing the ending of the word (second part) together with the final vowel of the first part (the root).

<u>With final Vowel</u>

Declension	2	1		2
Nominative singular	ος	η	α	ον
Genitive singular	ου	ης	ας	ου
Dative singular	ω	η	α	ω
Accusative singular	ον	ην	αν	ον
Nominative plural	οι	αι		<u>α</u>
Genitive plural	ων	ων		ων
Dative plural	οις	αις		οις
Accusative plural	ους	ας		<u>α</u>

Sticking with our example Greek word, which is a Noun in the second declension, is singular and is the object of the sentence, it can be seen that the first part (root) of that Noun can end in one of two vowels, namely 'η' or 'α' (note that vowels in Greek are not the same as the 5 in English).

The next table shows the full Greek words with their endings. The word in the first column is pronounced 'logos' and means 'word'. There are two words in the second column, the first is pronounced 'graphe' (meaning 'writing' or 'Scripture') and the second is pronounced 'oora' (meaning 'hour', 'occasion' or 'moment'). The word in the third column is pronounced 'ergon' and means 'work'.

Declension	2	1		2
Nominative singular	Λόγος	γραφή	ωρα	ἐργον
Genitive singular	Λόγου	γραφης	ωρας	ἐργου
Dative singular	Λόγω	γραφη	ωρα	ἐργω
Accusative singular	Λόγον	γραφήν	ωραν	ἐργον
Nominative plural	Λόγοι	γραφαι		ἐργα
Genitive plural	Λόγων	γραφων		ἐργων
Dative plural	Λόγοις	γραφαις		ἐργοις
Accusative plural	Λόγους	γραφας		ἐργα

The word 'Logos' in the first column is the Greek word used in John 1:1 when it says 'In the beginning was the Word' (logos). You can see from the table that the first part (root) of 'Logos' is 'Λόγ' (Log). It does not change whatever case the word is written in. However, the second part changes depending on the case, hence the word 'Logos' is actually the Greek word for 'word' when written in the Nominative singular case.

As an aside, it is worth noting that whenever you see a Greek word quoted in a dictionary or concordance such as Strongs, the word will always be shown in its Nominative singular form. Thus, if you look these words up in Strongs they will appear as Λόγος, γραφή, ωρα and ἐργον.

Now you may be asking what has all this got to do with Junia? To which the answer is to apply this information re Greek words above to the word for Junia which is underlined in the Greek text of Romans 16:7 above - 'ιουνιαν'

The first point to note is that the word ends with a 'ν'. From the tables we now know that this means the word is written in the Accusative case. But here's the thing. The ending of the word does not necessarily tell us whether the name is a woman's name or a man's name. Thus, when we look at the word 'ιουνιαν' we cannot tell if it is male or female. All we can tell is that the word is the object of the sentence.

There is another Greek convention, however, which does tell us whether a name is male or female. For the purposes of this study the technical nature of the convention is irrelevant. Suffice it to say that in Greek, if Junia is a man it will have a circumflex accent (^) on the 'α'. Hence it would look like this 'ιουνιᾶν'. However, if it is a woman, it will have an acute accent (´) on the 'ι', like this 'ιουνίαν' ^

Accordingly, all we have to do is look at the Bible, the Greek Bible, and see whether there's a circumflex accent on the 'α', making it a man, or an acute accent on the 'ι', making it a woman.

Except there is one problem with this. Unfortunately it was not until the ninth century AD, approximately 800 years after Paul wrote Romans that the Greeks started to write with accents on their words. So for the first 800 years from the time when Paul wrote Romans, what you actually see is this 'ιουνιαν', with no accent on the 'α' and no accent on the 'ι'.

And therefore, because from the name alone, the ending and the lack of accents, you cannot tell if it's a masculine or feminine name, you are left with an argument as to whether Junia was a man or a woman.

CHAPTER 6

The arguments against

According to my principle of scholarship it is essential that we correctly identify the arguments that are made in favour of the male name Junias and those which say you cannot tell whether it is male or female. Once identified, they should be accurately set out in order that they can then be properly tested.

It would be an impossible task to compile an exhaustive list of all the arguments that have ever been put forward against Junia being a woman. Rather than attempt the impossible, therefore, I have attempted to identify the most common and well known arguments, which I have done with reference to two prominent Complementarian books and a Complementarian website. For obvious reasons I have not included the argument that Junia cannot be a female apostle because elsewhere the Bible prohibits a woman holding such a position.

CBMW.

These initials stand for the Council for Biblical Manhood and Womanhood. And there is an article on that organisation's website which addresses the question of Junia. A copy of that article can be found online at http://cbmw.org/uncategorized/a-female-apostle/

The arguments in that article can be summarised as follows:

1. Older translators typically rendered the name in a masculine form;
2. The Accusative ending could be either masculine or feminine;
3. Throughout Church history, translators and commentators have been divided;
4. The majority of modern translations favour the masculine;
5. The Greek text of NA26 has a circumflex accent – masculine;

6. There are only two, possibly three occurrences of the name in Greek literature of the first century;
7. It is the shortened form of the male name Junianus;
8. Origen, early Church father, said it was a man;
9. Epiphanius, early Church father, said it was a man and knew more detail about him than is in the Bible;
10. Greek Minuscules from the 9th century onwards all accent the name as masculine.

Rather than take my word for it you should take the time to read the article yourself.

RBMW

These initials stand for the title of a book called 'Rediscovering Biblical Manhood and Womanhood'. Its editors were Wayne Grudem and John Piper and it contains a collection of chapters written by various authors, mainly male but including some by women. The issue of Junia is dealt with at pages 80 and 214. The name Junias is dealt with at pages 79, 80, 81, 214 and 221 and the name Junianus at pages 214 and 221. According to the index of that book, these names are not mentioned anywhere else in the main text, the only other references being in the footnotes section to the main pages.

Having carefully read all the references to Junia in this book (and Junias and Junianus), the arguments against Junia being a woman can be summarised as follows:

1. The evidence is indecisive;
2. A TLG search only revealed 3 results for the name Junia (ignoring Romans 16:7);
3. The Church Fathers were divided;
4. More significantly, a Latin quotation from Origen supports a masculine name;
5. It is a shortened form of a masculine name;
6. The name was not a common name in the Greek-speaking world.

EFBT

These initials stand for the title of a book called 'Evangelical Feminism and Biblical Truth' whose author was Wayne Grudem. According to the index the references to Junia are 220-227 and 526. The names Junias and Junianus do not appear in the index. Having carefully read all references to Junia in the book the arguments Grudem puts forward can be summarised as follows:

1. Just as in English, Chris or Pat could be a man's name or woman's name, so in Greek the name could be male or female;
2. There is little comment in the first 400 years of Church history and what comment there is, is mixed in respect of the gender;
3. The early Church Fathers were divided. Out of a list of 7 early Church Fathers, 5 said female and 2 (Origen and Epiphanius) said male;
4. It could be a shortened form of a man's name.

So there you have a total of 20 arguments. Some of them are repetitions because they are coming from different sources, but there are 20 arguments as to why either Junia was a man or, if not a man, why you cannot say with any sort of certainty that Junia was a woman. And if you can't say with certainty, it is suggested that it would be dangerous and unacceptable to try to shape your theology or to say that you interpret another verse of Scripture based on Junia being a woman apostle.

In the pages that follow I will deal with all 20 arguments. In doing so I intend to show that they are either plain wrong, disingenuous, overstated, or ill informed. I intend to show this not by bare assertion or expert opinion, but rather by presenting evidence, evidence that drives any objective and fair-minded person to conclude that it is completely and utterly wrong to say there is any doubt over whether Junia was a woman. We will then be in a position to turn our minds to the questions of whether the group referred to in Romans 16:7 were apostles or messengers and whether Junia was part of that group or known to them.

From this point on the arguments will be renumbered from 1 to 20 for ease of reference.

CBMW
1. Older translations typically rendered the name in a masculine form;
2. The Accusative ending could be either masculine or feminine;
3. Throughout Church history, translators and commentators have been divided;
4. The majority of modern translations favour the masculine;
5. The Greek text of NA26 has a circumflex accent – masculine;
6. There are only two, possibly three occurrences of the name in Greek literature of the first century;
7. It is the shortened form of the male name Junianus;
8. Origen, early Church father, said it was a man;
9. Epiphanius, early Church father, said it was a man and knew more detail about him than is in the Bible;
10. Greek Minuscules from the 9th century onwards all accent the name as masculine.

RBMW
11. The evidence is indecisive;
12. A TLG search only revealed 3 results for the name Junia (ignoring Romans 16:7);
13. The Church Fathers were divided;
14. More significantly, a Latin quotation from Origen supports a masculine name;
15. It is a shortened form of a masculine name;
16. The name was not a common name in the Greek-speaking world.

EFBT

17. Just as in English, Chris or Pat could be a man's name or woman's name, so in Greek the name could be male or female;

18. There is little comment in the first 400 years of Church history and what comment there is, is mixed in respect of the gender;

19. The early Church Fathers were divided. Out of a list of 7 early Church Fathers, 5 said female and 2 (Origen and Epiphanius) said male;

20. It could be a shortened form of a man's name.

Some readers may feel uncomfortable at being asked to disagree with the opinions of Greek scholars. After all, the arguments against Junia being a woman are put forward by very learned men, many of whom are professors of New Testament Greek. Indeed, some may question what right I have to disagree with them given my lack of any formal training in New Testament Greek. Such feelings and questions are easily answered.

Look carefully at the 20 arguments I have set out and then for the sake of argument let us concentrate on the first one. It states that the older translations typically rendered the name in a masculine form. The striking feature of that argument is that it amounts to a question of evidence. It has nothing to do with expert opinion or Greek scholarship. It is simply a statement of fact that is either true or false. We do not need the expert opinion of a Greek scholar to decide whether it is true, we just have to ask ourselves a simple evidential question; did the older translations typically render the name in the masculine form? If the evidence shows that they did, we should accept the statement as fact. But if the evidence shows that they did not we should reject the statement. They either did or they didn't, and you certainly do not need to be a Greek scholar to decide which it is.

What applies for the first argument applies to all the arguments. Go through them again and you will see that every single one of the 20 arguments is either a question of evidence and fact, or it is a conclusion drawn from evidence and fact. For example, consider argument 11 – the evidence is indecisive. That is very clearly a conclusion from the evidence. You simply need to look at the evidence and then decide whether it is indecisive or not. Another example would be argument 5 - the Greek text of NA 26 has a circumflex accent. It either does or it doesn't. You do not have to be a professor of Greek to decide that, you just need to know what a circumflex accent is and where the word is in the Greek text.

The point I wish to emphasise is that professors of Greek are no more qualified and have no more ability than you or I to consider questions of evidence and fact. They are all in the same boat as us. Together with them, we are equally entitled and able to look at the evidence and reach a conclusion. Granted, they may find it easier to find and understand the evidence, but once we non Greek Scholars are up to speed, once the evidence is presented and understood, our conclusions carry as much weight as theirs.

This takes me back to my guiding principles. Evidence decides arguments not the opinions of experts. Their opinions are highly informative and may well be right, but the crucial question is what evidence are they basing their opinions on? The quote from Robert Dick Wilson is worth repeating, in that I want to know when these professors write these books and who proclaim to be world experts on this subject, "where do they get their evidence from to start with?" I want to know if the evidence supports their views.

The answer to that question is set out in the following chapters, which deal with all 20 of the arguments set out above.

Chapter 7

Greek (and Latin) Literature

<u>CBMW</u>
1. Older translations typically rendered the name in a masculine form;
2. **The Accusative ending could be either masculine or feminine;**
3. Throughout Church history, translators and commentators have been divided;
4. The majority of modern translations favour the masculine;
5. The Greek text of NA26 has a circumflex accent – masculine;
6. **There are only two, possibly three occurrences of the name in Greek literature of the first century;**
7. It is the shortened form of the male name Junianus;
8. Origen, early Church father, said it was a man;
9. Epiphanius, early Church father, said it was a man and knew more detail about him than is in the Bible;
10. Greek Minuscules from the 9th century onwards all accent the name as masculine.

<u>RBMW</u>
11. **The evidence is indecisive;**
12. **A TLG search only revealed 3 results for the name Junia (ignoring Romans 16:7);**
13. The Church Fathers were divided;
14. More significantly, a Latin quotation from Origen supports a masculine name;
15. It is a shortened form of a masculine name;
16. **The name was not a common name in the Greek-speaking world.**

EFBT

17. **Just as in English, Chris or Pat could be a man's name or woman's name, so in Greek the name could be male or female;**
18. There is little comment in the first 400 years of Church history and what comment there is, is mixed in respect of the gender;
19. The early Church Fathers were divided. Out of a list of 7 early Church Fathers, 5 said female and 2 (Origen and Epiphanius) said male;
20. It could be a shortened form of a man's name.

Summary of arguments

These six arguments effectively amount to arguments for or from uncertainty. They are not positive arguments for Junia being a man, but rather they assert that because 1) the accusative ending could be either masculine or feminine; 2) the word is rare; and 3) the evidence is indecisive - it is impossible to say whether Junia was a man or a woman.

The argument that the evidence is indecisive is really a catch all argument, which applies to the whole question of whether Junia was a woman. For that reason I will deal with it more than once when looking at the evidence which relates to the other arguments.

Now, bear in mind that these arguments are from people that say one of two things; they either say this person was a man, or they say you can't say one way or the other. It's indecisive, so you cannot with all certainty say it's a woman. I reject those assertions. I intend to make a case for saying Junia was definitely a woman.

Arguments 2 and 17

As a matter of grammar the statement that says, it could be masculine or feminine is correct. We looked at the reasons for that in chapter 5. But in respect of whether Junia was a man or a woman that statement tells me nothing. Further, the statement is in fact misleading.

As a matter of English grammar, the names John, Allan or Steve could be masculine or feminine. There is no grammatical reason why Allan is a man's name. So saying that Junia could, as a matter of grammar, be male or female is the same as saying, Allan could, as a matter of grammar, be a girl's name. In short, the statement is meaningless. However, the statement is really saying what Grudem is saying at argument 17 in EFBT. Argument no 2 is saying implicitly what argument number 17 is saying explicitly, i.e. just as in English the names Chris or Pat can be male or female, so in Greek the name Junia can be male or female.

Not to put too fine a point on it, arguments 2 and 17 are at best disingenuous. Let us take a look at the evidence.

There is only one reason why we are able to say that in English Chris or Pat can be male or female and it has nothing to do with grammar. The reason Chris or Pat can be male or female is because you and I know from experience of men and women called Chris or Pat. I do not know of a woman called Allan and I do not know of a woman called John. Therefore, I do not accept that John or Allan can be a woman's name but I do accept Chris and Pat can.

Applying that to Junia, in order for arguments 2 and 17 to amount to anything more than meaningless statements, there has to be evidence of a man or men being called Junia. And that is where these arguments unravel, because it is a universally recognised and agreed fact, by people on both sides of the debate, that there is not a single instance in any Greek literature (by which I mean any

32

Greek literature in all the searches over hundreds and hundreds of years from 500 years before Paul wrote Romans to several hundred years after he wrote Romans) of a man called Junia - not a single one.

Given the complete lack of evidence of any man having been called Junia, the question arises as to the basis on which a professor considered it appropriate to go to print with an assertion that, just as in English, Chris or Pat can be male or female, so in Greek Junia can be male or female? What possible evidential basis has he got for saying that? Void of a single shred of supporting evidence, arguments 2 and 17 are completely without merit.

Arguments 6, 12 and 16

Arguments 6 and 12 are making an identical point but worded slightly differently. Both are basing their assertion on the same search of Greek literature, its just that argument 12 identifies that search (TLG) whereas argument 6 does not.

The question naturally arises as to what is 'TLG'.

TLG are the initials taken from the name 'Thesaurus Linguae Graecae'. It is a research centre, which is based at the University of California. I know this because it says so on the TLG website! You can find more detail at www.tlg.uci.edu/ but the following is an abridged version of the 'about us' page on that website.

> "Founded in 1972 the TLG represents the first effort in the Humanities to produce a large digital corpus of literary texts. Since its inception the project has collected and digitized most texts written in Greek from Homer (8 c. B.C.) to the fall of Byzantium in AD 1453 and beyond. Its goal is to create a comprehensive digital library of Greek literature from antiquity to the present era.

In spring 2001 the TLG-team developed its own search engine and made the corpus available online. Today the Online TLG contains more than 105 million words from over 10,000 works associated with 4,000 authors and is constantly updated and improved with new features and texts. The full corpus is available to more than 2,000 subscribing institutions and thousands of individuals in 58 countries worldwide.

A subcorpus (Abridged TLG) together with the extensive bibliographical database developed by the TLG (Canon of Greek Authors and Works) is open to the public. The Abridged version contains 900 Greek works from 67 authors and uses the same search engine as the full Online TLG version. It provides access to the most important classical authors and a large number of patristic texts. "

Arguments 6 and 12 are simply stating that when a search of the TLG database was carried out it provided only three results for the name Junia. Details of this search are set out at page 79 of RBMW. Based on this result argument 16 states that the name was not common in the Greek-speaking world.

The first point to make about the TLG search is that there is no dispute that on the three occasions Junia was found, they were speaking of a woman. It is also interesting to note the search parameters, namely around 9th Century BC to 5th Century AD. I have been unable to find any explanation from either Grudem or Piper for this date range. This is significant because if you widen the date range by a few hundred years (i.e. extend it to the 7th Century AD) you get a total of 7 instances of Junia, more than double the number of results quoted in RBMW.

But there is a more fundamental flaw in the argument relating to the TLG search. It is universally accepted, by people on both sides of the debate, that Junia is a Latin name. The TLG search was only in respect of Greek literature. It was therefore searching for a Latin name in Greek literature, which makes it hardly surprising that a relatively small number of instances of the name occurring was found. It is even more surprising that this small number is then used to advance an argument for uncertainty as to whether Junia is a man or woman's name. This would be akin to carrying out a search of English literature for a French name, finding only three instances of it and thus declaring that it was an uncommon name. It may well be uncommon in England, but that tells us nothing of its usage in France. Similarly, Junia may have been a relatively uncommon name in the Greek-speaking world, but in the Latin world it was very common. A point all the more important when we remember that we are dealing with a name in the book of Romans, written to the Church in Rome.

Common sense dictates that if you want to know the frequency, or in our case the gender of a Latin name, you carry out a search of Latin literature. Not surprisingly, such searches have been carried out and they reveal two important findings. First, there are literally hundreds of instances of the name Junia. Secondly, in every single one of those instances the person referred to was a woman. These two points are so important that they bear repeating. There are hundreds of instances of the name Junia in Latin literature and in every single one of them Junia is a woman. Put another way, there is not a single instance in the hundreds of references in Latin literature of Junia ever being a man's name.

Conclusion

So, in conclusion, arguments 2 and 17 are irrelevant. They are no different to saying that as a matter of English grammar John or Allan could be a man or a woman. On the other hand what is relevant, is that just as in English there is no evidence of John being a woman's name, so in Greek and Latin there is no evidence of Junia being a man's name.

Arguments 6, 12 and 16 fail as well. Rather than create the intended uncertainty, they in fact strengthen the case for Junia being a woman by demonstrating that not a single instance has ever been found in Greek or Latin literature of Junia being a man's name. And of course argument 16 tells us nothing because Junia is not a Greek name.

All five arguments feed into argument 11 and are used to support the assertion that the evidence is indecisive. This implies that the evidence goes both ways. But when the evidence is examined this proves not to be the case. The evidence from Greek and Latin literature only goes one way, it never points in favour of Junia being a man. If such overwhelmingly one-sided evidence can properly be described as indecisive, I venture to suggest our criminal justice system would cease to function. There would be no prospect of anyone ever being convicted of any offence. The simple fact is that it is nonsense to suggest the evidence is indecisive. It is not indecisive, it is overwhelmingly in favour of a female name and there is not a shred of evidence in Greek or Latin literature of Junia being a male name - ever.

Those arguments having failed to stand up to the lightest of examinations, they must be removed from the list. Accordingly the list of arguments against Junia being a woman now looks like this:

CBMW
1. Older translators typically rendered the name in a masculine form;
2.
3. Throughout Church history, translators and commentators have been divided;
4. The majority of modern translations favour the masculine;
5. The Greek text of NA26 has a circumflex accent – masculine;
6.
7. It is the shortened form of the male name Junianus;
8. Origen, early Church father, said it was a man;

9. Epiphanius, early Church father, said it was a man and knew more detail about him than is in the Bible;
10. Greek Minuscules from the 9th century onwards all accent the name as masculine.

RBMW

11.
12.
13. The Church Fathers were divided;
14. More significantly, a Latin quotation from Origen supports a masculine name;
15. It is a shortened form of a masculine name;
16.

EFBT

17.
18. There is little comment in the first 400 years of Church history and what comment there is, is mixed in respect of the gender;
19. The early Church Fathers were divided. Out of a list of 7 early Church Fathers, 5 said female and 2 (Origen and Epiphanius) said male;
20. It could be a shortened form of a man's name.

The more prescient reader may be able to form a fairly accurate idea as to what this list will end up looking like.

Chapter 8

The Early Church Fathers

CBMW
1. Older translations typically rendered the name in a masculine form;
2.
3. **Throughout Church history, translators and commentators have been divided;**
4. The majority of modern translations favour the masculine;
5. The Greek text of NA26 has a circumflex accent – masculine;
6.
7. It is the shortened form of the male name Junianus;
8. **Origen, early Church father, said it was a man;**
9. **Epiphanius, early Church father, said it was a man and knew more detail about him than is in the Bible;**
10. Greek Minuscules from the 9th century onwards all accent the name as masculine.

RBMW
11.
12.
13. **The Church Fathers were divided;**
14. **More significantly, a Latin quotation from Origen supports a masculine name;**
15. It is a shortened form of a masculine name;
16.

EFBT
17.
18. **There is little comment in the first 400 years of Church history and what comment there is, is mixed in respect of the gender;**
19. **The early Church Fathers were divided. Out of a list of 7 early Church Fathers, 5 said female and 2 (Origen and Epiphanius) said male;**
20. It could be a shortened form of a man's name

Here you have seven arguments which all relate, at least in part, to the early Church Fathers. Thus the question immediately arises, what is so relevant about the early Church Fathers?

When people speak of the early Church Fathers, they are referring to prominent people in the Church who lived from around the time of the New Testament onwards. As Paul wrote Romans in the 1st Century AD, many of these early Church Fathers were only a few hundred years removed from the time of his writing. One very well known early Church father is Origen, who is one of the earliest of the Church Fathers (3rd Century AD).

You may recall that it was not until the 9th Century AD that accents were added to Greek words when they were being written and that those accents can tell us whether a name is male or female (circumflex accent = male, acute accent = female). As the book of Romans was written without any accents, highly relevant evidence can be obtained from looking at the writings of the early Church Fathers. Many of those Church Fathers wrote what we might today call commentaries, and in their writings they wrote about the verse in Romans 16 where the name Junia appears. It is therefore highly relevant evidence to see if in their writings they referred to Junia as a man or as a woman.

As their writings were before the 9th Century and thus without accents, the same problem applies. However, unlike with the biblical passage in Romans 16:7, we are able to look at the context of the writings of the Church Fathers to see if they are treating Junia as a man's name or a woman's name.

An example about context will hopefully make the point. Imagine that you were living at a point in the future, say, 500 years from now. Being interested in history and in particular English history of the 21st Century, you decide to look at some English literature which is kept in a local museum and which historians have dated to the 21st Century. When you examine that literature you come across the name 'John', which is a name you have never heard of because people stopped calling their children John towards the end of the 21st Century. You therefore have no personal knowledge as to whether John is a man's name or a woman's name. However, upon reading the sentence in which the word 'John' appears you see that it reads 'John walked slowly to the door, dragging his feet as he went'. Now, by looking at the context in which the name 'John' appears you are able to say with certainty that it is referring to a man, not a woman. This is because the pronouns 'his' and 'he' which appear later in the sentence are clearly referring to John, they are masculine pronouns and therefore John must be masculine.

In the same way we can look at the context of references to Junia in the writings of the early Church Fathers to see whether they were referring to Junia as a man or a woman. One such reference appears in the writings of a Church father called Chrysostom. Writing in his native tongue of Greek and when talking about the Junia who is mentioned in Romans 16:7 he says this: 'how great the wisdom of this woman must have been that she was deemed worthy of the title of 'apostle'. Thus, by the use of the words 'woman' and 'she' we are left in no doubt that Chrysostom considered the person named in Romans 16:7 to be a woman.

The arguments in respect of the early Church Fathers are really asserted in support of the contention that the evidence is indecisive. It is said that the opinions and writings of the early Church Fathers was divided, some thought Junia was a woman, others a man. Thus, it is asserted, you cannot reach any definitive position based on the writings of the early Church Fathers.

Arguments 3, 8, 9, 13, 14, 18 and 19

Although it is not immediately apparent from the wording of arguments 3, 13 and 18, it is apparent from arguments 8, 9, 14 and 19 that two early Church Fathers are claimed to have referred to Junia as being a man, and those two are Origen and Epiphanius. In respect of Epiphanius, it is stated that his writings include information about Junia which is not found in the biblical text of Romans 16:7. Thus, it is said, he must have had personal knowledge of Junia and therefore his writings should carry more evidential weight.

So what do we make of Origen and Epiphanius?

Origen

Origen was Greek and therefore not unnaturally his writings were in Greek. However, when references are made to Origen they are in fact made to Latin translations of his Greek writings. Arguments 18 and 19 come from Grudem's book EFBT and he deals with the question of Origen and Junia at page 225. When Grudem cites Origen as referring to Junia as a man, he cites a Latin translation of Origen's writings. To be fair to Grudem, he does acknowledge that there is some dispute over the translation and he is aware that some have asserted this reference to be a mistranslation. However, in response to those assertions he says he has been 'unable independently to evaluate the evidence for that claim'.

I have to say I find Grudem's statement a little surprising. He has produced a book which runs to over 800 pages and which clearly required a great deal of research. He has cited a reference to Origen in support of one of his arguments but is aware that that reference is disputed. Surely, in those circumstances, it is incumbent on him to make the time and every effort 'independently to evaluate the evidence for that claim'?

Grudem's statement is also disappointing, because if he had made the time and effort it might have saved him from making an incorrect statement. He would have been able to establish that his reference to Origen is wrong. It is a mistranslation and contrary to what Grudem asserts, Origen in fact referred to Junia as a woman.

Origen in fact referred to Junia in two places in his commentary, the first being in the section where he deals with verse 7 in chapter 16, the second coming in a later passage where he is discussing the people with whom Paul shared a racial heritage. Junia comes up in that discussion because when Paul refers to Junia in Romans 16:7 he refers to Junia (and Andronicus) as his 'kinsmen'.

When you look at the first passage, the main discussion about Junia, it is clear that Origen refers to her as a woman. It is only in the later passage that there can be any suggestion Origen referred to her as a man.

What then is the reason for Grudem's reference to the later passage? The answer is quite straightforward. Origen's writings were translated into Latin and many ancient manuscripts still exist showing this Latin translation. Those manuscripts were written or translated by various people over a period spanning many hundreds of years. The majority of those manuscripts refer to Junia as a woman. However, there are two manuscripts, which are said to originate from the late 12th Century, which, in the later discussion about the people with whom Paul shared a racial heritage, refer to Junia as a man. It is beyond doubt that this is a mistranslation.

Indeed, it is of interest to note that other Greek scholars, whose paper Grudem relies on to support his translation in the ESV Bible of 'known to the apostles', accept that the Origen reference to Junia being a man is a mistranslation and accept that Origen in fact referred to Junia as being a woman. That paper is considered in detail in chapters 13-23, but suffice it to say for now that the authors of that paper confirm they have examined the issue of Origen's reference to Junia and are satisfied that the reference to Junia being a man is a mistranslation.

Epiphanius

Grudem and Piper refer to Epiphanius at page 79 of RMBW. There, in the main text of the book, they state the following:

> *"Epiphanius (AD 315-402), the bishop of Salamis in Cyprus, wrote an Index of Disciples, in which he*

> *includes this line: "[Junias], of whom Paul makes mention, became bishop of Apameia of Syria" (Index disciplulorum, 125.19-20). In Greek, the phrase "of whom" is a masculine relative pronoun (hou) and shows that Epiphanius thought [Junias] was a man"*

There is no footnote at the end of that paragraph. It is followed by a paragraph dealing with Chrysostom, at the end of which there is a footnote (no.18). Having set out the positions of Epiphanius and Chrysostom they go on in the next paragraph to say:

> *"Perhaps somewhat more weight may be given to the statement by Epiphanius, since he appears to know more specific information about Junias (that he became bishop of Apameia), while Chrysostom gives no more information than what we could deduce from Romans 16:7"*

At the end of that paragraph, after the reference to 'Romans 16:7' there is a footnote (no.19). The text of that footnote appears on page 479, almost exactly 400 pages removed from the main text it is referring to. That footnote reads:

> *"However, we are perplexed about the fact that in the neat context of the citation concerning Junias, Epiphanius also designates Prisca as a man mentioned in Romans 16:3, even though we know from the New Testament that she is a woman."*

Two questions arise from this. First, why was this footnote (which undermines the credibility of Epiphanius) not included in the main text? And secondly, why do they consider it proper to suggest more weight should be given to Epiphanius because he apparently knows more about Junia than is written in Romans, without at the same time drawing the reader's attention to him being unable correctly to identify the gender of Prisca?

So, just to clarify. It is correct to state that Epiphanius referred to Junia as a man. As the Origen reference has been refuted, that leaves Epiphanius as the sole Church father who ever referred to Junia as a man. However, in considering how much if any weight we should attach to Epiphanius' evidence we have to take into account the fact that he also referred to Prisca (Priscilla) as a man. Unlike with Junia, there is no argument about whether the Prisca he was referring to was a man or a woman because, unlike with Junia, the New Testament itself expressly tells us that Prisca was a woman.

The simple fact is that the only early Church father witness who can be called in support of the argument for a man is somewhat discredited by the fact he was unable correctly to identify Prisca as a woman.

Does that strike you as ambiguous, indecisive or 50/50?

Other Church Fathers

Some Egalitarian writers have given lists of which early Church Fathers said Junia was a woman. Some list only Greek Church Fathers, others include Latin. Most if not all like to quote Chrysostom, which in full reads: 'To be an apostle is something great but to be outstanding among the apostles, just think what a wonderful sum of praise that is. Indeed, how great the wisdom of this woman must have been that she was deemed worthy of the title of apostle.' We will revisit that quote in chapter 12 when we come to consider what evidential weight should be given to the writings of a fourth century Greek scholar, who spoke Greek as his mother tongue, and who considered the Greek of Romans 16:7 to be referring to an apostle as opposed to a messenger.

I do not intend to reproduce the lists of Church Fathers; I just refer to them in order to make one point. Epiphanius aside, there is not a single Church father, writing in Greek or Latin, in the 1,000 years immediately following Paul's writing the book of Romans, who refers to Junia as a man. Again, that point is so important it bears repeating. Every single Church father in the first millennium, writing in Greek or Latin who referred to the Junia of Romans 16:7 referred to her as a woman, the one exception being Epiphanius.

It is also quite informative to consider some of the comments those Church Fathers made about Junia. One called Theodoret referred to Junia as 'called of note not only among the disciples but also among the teachers, and not just among the teachers but even among the apostles'. John of Damascus, speaking of Junia said 'to be called apostles is a great thing, but to be even amongst these of note, just consider what a great encomium that is.'

As to the Latin Fathers, not only do they refer to Junia as being a woman, but some of them discuss and opine that Junia was probably one of the 72 that we read about in the Gospels as having been commissioned and sent out.

To complete the picture, it is not in fact until you get to around the 13th Century that, Epiphanius aside, you find the first reference to Junia being a man. Jumping forward to the 16th Century, a certain Martin Luther referred to Junia as being a man, but Erasmus, on whose Greek text the King James Bible was based, referred to Junia as a woman, hence the name Junia in the King James Bible and not Junias.

Arguments 3 and 18

This argument rather depends on what is meant by Church history. As we have just seen, there was no such division in the first 1,200 years or so of Church history. If this argument is including or referring to the first 1,200 years of Church history then it is quite simply wrong.

It is also wrong to state that there is little comment in the first 400 years and that it is mixed. There is in fact considerable comment during the first 1,000 years and none of it is mixed.

Conclusion

All 7 arguments simply do not stand up to scrutiny. Church history and the writings of the Church Fathers speak loudly and clearly of the Junia of Romans 16:7 being a woman.

Which leaves our list of arguments looking like this:

CBMW
1. Older translations typically rendered the name in a masculine form;
2.
3.
4. The majority of modern translations favour the masculine;
5. The Greek text of NA26 has a circumflex accent – masculine;
6.
7. It is the shortened form of the male name Junianus;
8.
9.
10. Greek Minuscules from the 9th century onwards all accent the name as masculine.

RBMW
11.
12.
13.
14.
15. It is a shortened form of a masculine name;
16.

<u>EFBT</u>

    17.

    18.

    19.

    20. It could be a shortened form of a man's name.

Chapter 9

Greek New Testament

CBMW
1. Older translations typically rendered the name in a masculine form;
2.
3.
4. The majority of modern translations favour the masculine;
5. **The Greek text of NA26 has a circumflex accent – masculine;**
6.
7. It is the shortened form of the male name Junianus;
8.
9.
10. **Greek Minuscules from the 9th century onwards all accent the name as masculine.**

RBMW
11.
12.
13.
14.
15. It is a shortened form of a masculine name;
16.

EFBT
17.
18.
19.
20. It could be a shortened form of a man's name.

We now come to arguments from the Greek New Testament. These two are positive arguments in favour of Junia being a man. As has previously been explained, a circumflex accent on the 'α' of Junia indicates that Junia was a man. However, accents were not added to Greek words until around the 9th Century, so prior to that date it was impossible to tell just from looking at the word whether Junia was speaking of a man or a woman.

Textual History

It is important at this point to consider the subject of textual history.

As a starting point, it is common ground that none of the original documents on which the New Testament books were first written is in existence today. So, the original document on which Paul or someone on his behalf wrote the book of Romans does not exist. However, whilst no original document has survived, we do have an abundance of copies (manuscripts). These copies come from different parts of the world and from different points in history. It is impossible to say how many generations removed from the original documents these copies are; by which I mean it is logically possible that one or more of them could have been copied directly from the original, whereas others could be copies of copies of copies of copies.

Those copies, which were made nearest in time to the original, were written in what we might call capital letters. They are known as 'majuscules'. As this way of writing pre-dated the 9th Century, the words in those copies were written without any accents. As time progressed, copies began to be written in what we would call lowercase. These copies are known as 'minuscules'.

It is a fact of life that no-one is perfect, and the people who used to hand write the majuscules and minuscules were no exception. Thus, when you look at all the various copies, when you compare them with each other, although they may be virtually identical, there are bound to be the odd differences. There may be a missing word, an additional word, a missing letter or a misspelt word. In short, there are copying errors.

Now, when you look at the full textual tradition, sometimes you'll see that words are changed when they are copied, and that can be a clue as to the meaning or context of the original word. The Junia of Romans 16:7 is no exception, in that the textual tradition shows that some copies have written the name differently. However, it is interesting to note that Junia has only ever been wrongly copied one way, or what textual critics refer to as a 'variant'. There are some copies which have the name 'Julia' instead of 'Junia'. Thus, it is said, there is only one textual variant of Romans 16:7, that being Julia. What makes this interesting for us is that rather like John in English, there is no question mark over the gender of the name 'Julia'. Scholarly opinion is united in the view that Julia is a woman's name. This means that the only textual variant for Romans 16:7 has the person named as a woman.

The textual variant of Julia is not of course determinative of the arguments. However, it does mean that certain copyists thought that the person named in Romans 16:7 was a woman.

The real question for us, which relates to the textual tradition is; what happened from the ninth century onwards? Because from the ninth century onwards we have Greek texts with accents and that means we can look at Romans 16:7 in those texts to see if they wrote a man's name (circumflex accent) or a woman's name (acute accent); that brings us to arguments 5 and 10.

Arguments 5 and 10

I will come straight to the point. Argument 5 is correct. Argument 10 is wrong. It is correct to state that the Greek text of NA 26, which I will deal with shortly, has a circumflex accent. However, in respect of the Greek minuscules from the ninth century onwards, it is just plain wrong to state that they all accent the name as masculine. Just to be clear, I am not saying argument 10 is ambiguous, I am not saying it is indecisive; I am saying it is wrong.

NA26

The facts relating to NA26 are highly informative and are perhaps the best example of why it is so important to remember that evidence wins arguments, not the opinions of experts. With NA 26 we have as clear a case as you are ever likely to see of the experts getting it wrong.

The obvious place to start is to answer the question; what is NA26?

The following is an abridged version of the history page of the NA website at http://www.nestle-aland.com/en/the-28-edition/

> *"In 1898 Eberhard Nestle published the first edition of his Novum Testamentum Graece (New Testament Greek). Nestle took the three leading scholarly editions of the Greek New Testament at that time by Tischendorf, Westcott/Hort and Weymouth as a basis. Where their textual decisions differed from each other Nestle chose for his own text the variant which was preferred by two of the editions included, while the variant of the third was put into the apparatus.*
>
> *The text-critical apparatus remained rudimentary in all the editions published by Eberhard Nestle. It was Eberhard Nestle's son Erwin who provided the 13th edition of 1927 with a consistent critical apparatus showing evidence from manuscripts, early translations and patristic citations.*
>
> *In the nineteen-fifties Kurt Aland started working for the edition and introduced a method of checking the apparatus entries against Greek manuscripts and editions of the Church Fathers. This phase came to a close in 1963 when the 25th edition of the Novum Testamentum Graece appeared; later printings of this*

edition already carried the brand name "Nestle-Aland" on their covers.

The 26th edition, which appeared in 1979, featured a fundamentally new approach. Until then the guiding principle had been to adopt the text supported by a majority of the critical editions referred to. Now the text was established on the basis of source material that had been assembled and evaluated in the intervening period. It included early papyri and other manuscript discoveries, so that the 26th edition represented the situation of textual criticism in the 20th century.

Its text was identical with that of the 3rd edition of the UBS Greek New Testament (GNT) published in 1975, as a consequence of the parallel work done on both editions.

The first edition of the GNT appeared in 1966. Its text was established along the lines of Westcott and Hort and differed considerably from Nestle's 25th edition. This holds true for the second edition of the GNT as well. When the third edition was prepared Kurt Aland was able to contribute the textual proposals coming from his preliminary work on the 26th edition of the Nestle-Aland. Hence the process of establishing the text for both editions continued to converge, so that eventually they could share an identical text. However, their external appearance and the design of their apparatus remain different, because they serve different purposes. The GNT is primarily intended for translators, providing a reliable Greek initial text and a text-critical apparatus showing variants that are relevant for translation. The Novum Testamentum Graece is produced primarily for research, academic education and pastoral practice. It seeks to provide an apparatus that enables the reader to make a critical assessment of the reconstruction of the Greek initial text."

So, in summary, the title NA is taken from the surnames of Messrs Nestle and Aland. The 26 simply refers to the edition. It is a Greek Text that seeks to show what the editors consider to be the most accurate representation of the original.

Textual tradition again

To understand the significance of NA26 we need to return to the subject of the textual tradition and 'variants'. No original New Testament text is in existence today, i.e. the original manuscript on which the author wrote the New Testament book or letter. However, there are copies, and in various libraries and institutions around the world there are literally thousands of Greek New Testament manuscripts. Some contain the whole of the New Testament as we know it, others might appear to be nothing more than small scraps of paper, which contain only a few verses of a particular book of the New Testament. Over many years and with painstaking research, scholars have collated various records of these manuscripts.

These historical manuscripts are interesting for a number of reasons, but for present purposes their significance relates to the issues of 'variants'. These manuscripts are not identical. Whilst major sections of their text may perfectly match the same sections in other manuscripts, it is also the case that there are differences. On every occasion where there is a difference, the textual critic has to make a decision as to which version to go with. Factors, which may influence that decision, will be the age of the manuscripts and how many manuscripts support a particular reading.

For example, if out of 100 manuscripts, 97 support one reading and only 3 support an alternative reading, the textual critic may decide that the reading that is supported by the 97 is to be preferred. However, against this it may be the case that the 3 that support the alternative reading are the oldest, perhaps only a few hundred years after the date of the original text itself, whereas the 97 may all date to a period over 1,000 years after the original text. Now the textual critic might think that more weight should be given to the older manuscripts, as there has been less time between them and the original text for copying errors to creep in, whereas the 97 have had over 1,000 years for copying errors to occur.

Sticking with our example 100 manuscripts, it may be that at another part of the New Testament they vary in different ways. At this second location it may be that 75 of them support one reading, 20 support another and the remaining 5 support a third reading. Now you have manuscripts that were previously in agreement on the first occasion, but are now in disagreement over a different part of the text. Again, the textual critic has to decide which variant to prefer.

It does not take very long to realise that textual criticism can get very complicated indeed. It is a fascinating discipline, however, and I would highly recommend further reading on it. For present purposes we do not need to explore it in any more detail, but we do need to note some important principles.

1. No original manuscript exists.
2. Thousands of copies exist.
3. The copies are not identical.
4. Whenever there is a place in the text where the copies differ, the textual critic has to decide which copy to prefer.

You can see the result of textual criticism if you open your Bible to look at a famous passage in the gospels – the Lord's prayer. Literally millions of people around the world are able to recite the Lord's prayer, but I suspect most would be very surprised to be told by some textual critics that they are getting the words wrong.

The passage in question occurs in two of the gospels, namely Matthew and Luke. In Matthew it commences at verse 9 of

Chapter 6, in Luke at verse 2 of Chapter 11. To illustrate the point of textual criticism, here are verses 2-4 of chapter 11 in Luke, first from the King James Version (KJV) and then from the English Standard Version (ESV).

KJV

And he said unto them, When ye pray, say, Our Father which art in heaven, Hallowed be thy name. Thy kingdom come. Thy will be done, as in heaven, so in earth. [3] Give us day by day our daily bread. [4] And forgive us our sins; for we also forgive every one that is indebted to us. And lead us not into temptation; but deliver us from evil.

ESV

And he said to them, "When you pray, say: "Father, hallowed be your name. Your kingdom come. [3] Give us each day our daily bread, [4] and forgive us our sins, for we ourselves forgive everyone who is indebted to us. And lead us not into temptation."

The differences between the two versions are quite striking and textual criticism is the reason for them. In short, the editors of the ESV have based their translation on different manuscripts than those on which the KJV was based.

NA26 again

This brings us back to NA26. In short, it is an attempt at reconstructing the original Greek text of the New Testament by putting together all the preferred readings wherever there is a difference in the available copies. Because of the distinguished scholars behind the NA text, it is widely regarded as the most authoritative Greek New Testament text in the world today. It is certainly the case that the various editions of the NA text have been used as the basis for the vast majority of modern Bible translations in the course of the last 100 years. And for the reasons explained in the history section from the NA website, the UBS text is held in similarly high regard.

As stated above, argument 5 is correct. NA26 does have a circumflex accent on the name in Romans 16:7. Accordingly, the most authoritative Greek text of its day, compiled with reference to thousands of Greek manuscripts and representing the views of the world's leading experts on the Greek New Testament, makes a very clear statement that Junia was a man.

Faced with such overwhelming expert opinion there is only one question to ask. In the words of Robert Dick Wilson:

> *"I wish to know who the [experts] are and why they agree. Where do they get their evidence from to start with? My point is that you ought to be able to trace back this agreement amongst [experts] to the original [expert] who propounded the statement and then find out whether what that [expert] said is true. What was the foundation of his statement?"*

Evidence v Experts

In order to understand the fallacy of argument 5, we first need to look at argument 10. It is an unambiguous statement of fact about the accenting of all the minuscules from the 9th Century onwards. It asserts that they all show a man's name – a circumflex accent.

I too am making an unambiguous statement of fact about the very same thing. I am asserting that they all show a woman's name – an acute accent. One of us has to be wrong.

If argument 10 is really wrong, the question has to be asked why or how someone could make such a mistake? Why would someone say all the minuscules are accented with a circumflex accent if they are not? To answer that question we need to do some detective work and follow a paper trail.

Argument 10 is made in the CBMW article. That article contains a number of footnotes, of which three (nos. 13, 54 and 55) refer to this argument. Indeed, at footnote 55 the author criticizes another person (Richard Cervin) for having written about Junia but failing to acknowledge that the manuscripts from the 9th Century were all accented as masculine.

On looking at these three footnotes more carefully, it is apparent that they all refer back to a book by Fitzmyer. The book in question has in some circles been described as a 'magisterial commentary' on the book of Romans. The book was published in 1993, a not insignificant date, as we shall shortly see.

It is safe to assume that Fitzmyer was carrying out the research for his book in the years leading up to its publication in 1993. If one cross references this date with the past editions of the NA Greek New Testament, you will see that in 1993 the then current edition was number 26, thus NA26. Further cross-referencing will show that the then current edition of the UBS Greek New Testament was number 3, thus UBS3.

If you open a NA Greek New Testament you will see that it has what is known as the main text together with what is called a 'critical apparatus'. The way this works in practise is that where there is a choice between two or more possible readings of the Greek Text (variants), the main text will contain the preferred reading, the one the authors consider to be most likely to represent the original reading. If there is an alternative reading with some textual support, it will be shown in the critical apparatus.

A good analogy would be the treatment of Romans 16:7 in the ESV Bible. In the main text the word 'apostle' appears, but there is a footnote which tells you that the word 'messenger' is an alternative reading. Because the editors of the ESV consider 'apostle' to be the more likely translation, that word appears in the main text. However, as they also consider there to be some support for the alternative translation of 'messenger', that word appears in the footnote, the equivalent of the critical apparatus in the NA Greek New Testament.

Turning back to the NA Greek New Testament, it is a matter of historical record that edition number 13 (NA13) came out in 1927. It is also a matter of historical record that from NA13 to NA25, which came out in 1963, the main text had a circumflex accent over the 'α' of Junia in Romans 16:7. At the same time, in the critical apparatus they all included the alternative possibility that Junia was in fact a woman, i.e. an acute accent over the 'ι'.

NA26 came out in 1979. As with all previous editions from NA13 onwards, NA26 had Junia in the main text with a circumflex accent over the 'α'. However, there was a significant change in the critical apparatus of NA26, as for the first time it parted company with the previous editions and removed any reference to the possibility of Junia being a woman.

UBS3 came out in 1975. Like NA26, it too had Junia in the text as being a man. Another characteristic of UBS3 was that it would list the evidence in support of its preferred reading of the Greek text. Thus, in support of its reading that there was a circumflex accent on the 'α' of Junia in Romans 16:7, it listed a number of manuscripts. In fact, it listed 8 majuscules and a further 22 minuscules, all cited in support of Junia having a circumflex accent on the 'α'.

At this point the more alert reader will have spotted an obvious problem with UBS3. As has already been explained, the only way to tell from looking at the word whether Junia is a man or woman is to see if it has a circumflex accent (man) or an acute accent (woman). By citing a total of 30 manuscripts, UBS3 was asserting that those 30 manuscripts all had a circumflex accent over the 'α' in the word Junia in Romans 16:7. As there is no other way in which any of them could support the male reading there can be no other reason to cite them in support.

As we know, accents were not added to Greek manuscripts until the 9th century. It follows that all 30 manuscripts in UBS3 would have to have been written from the 9th Century onwards. But this is not the case. The 8 majuscules (capital letters) listed in UBS3 were all written prior to the 9th century and all of them were written without accents. The rather obvious question therefore arises as to on what basis a manuscript without accents can be cited in support of a reading with a circumflex accent? Absent accents, those 8 manuscripts can tell us nothing about the gender of the name in Romans 16:7. Accordingly, the citation of 8 majuscules in support of a masculine reading must be ignored.

That takes us to the 22 minuscules. Here the problem of no accent is avoided because these manuscripts were all written with accents. Thus, at best UBS3 can only rely on the 22 minuscules in support of a masculine reading.

As stated above, NA26 and UBS3 were the then current editions of the respective Greek New Testaments in the build up to 1993, when Fitzmyer published his commentary on Romans. In that commentary Fitzmyer states that all the minuscules from the 9th century onwards have the masculine accent on the word Junia in Romans 16:7. Hence, the author of the CBMW article cites Fitzmyer in support of his assertion that this is the case (argument 10).

Whilst there is no conclusive proof, it would appear most likely that Fitzmyer's source for his assertion were the then current editions of NA26 and UBS3. Thus the paper trail from the CBMW article goes from CBMW to Fitzmyer and then from Fitzmyer to NA26 and UBS3. Fitzmyer knew that NA26 and UBS3 represented the very best expert opinions on the subject. Further, unlike with previous editions, NA26 would not even have alerted

Fitzmyer to the possible alternative reading of a woman's name because reference to this in the critical apparatus had been removed.

At this point you will need to cast your mind back to the guiding principles set out at the beginning of this book, in particular the ones relating to evidence and expert opinion. I will never tire of repeating the quote from Robert Dick Wilson, which when applied to the subject of NA26 and UBS3 would produce a statement like this:

I want to trace back to the first person who said it. In this case, it's not the author of the CBMW article, he's quoting Fitzmyer. Its not Fitzmyer, as he's probably quoting from NA26 and UBS3. Therefore, I want to know why did the editors of NA26 and UBS3 say it? What did they base their evidence on?

Before answering that question we need to complete the paper trail, as it does not finish with NA26 and UBS3. A few years after Fitzmyer's commentary was published, the next edition of the NA Greek New Testament came out, not surprisingly known as NA27. There was also a new edition of the UBS Greek New Testament, again not surprisingly known as UBS4. In fact this was published in 1993, the same year as Fitzmyer's commentary, but in 1998, there was a jubilee edition fifth printing of NA27 and a third printing of UBS4.

So now, some 5 years after Fitzmyer's commentary came out, we have two new editions - NA27 and UBS4. And there was a very surprising and informative change in the way they dealt with Romans 16:7

I'll come straight to the point. In the main text of NA27 and UBS4 they both have an acute accent over the 'ι' in the name Junia in Romans 16:7. Even more surprisingly, when you look at the critical apparatus you will see that it says nothing about any alternative reading. In short, there is a complete reversal of the situation as it appeared in NA26, although it is more than a complete reversal because instead of just switching the main text and the critical apparatus, the reading from the critical apparatus has been moved to the main text, but the previous reading from the main text has disappeared altogether. Put another way, the preferred reading in NA26 is not even considered a possible reading in NA27.

This raises the immediate question as to why this volte-face has happened. The answer is provided by looking at the evidence cited in UBS4 in support of the preferred reading, where we find another surprise.

Just as with the previous edition, UBS4 cites a number of manuscripts in support of its preferred reading, i.e. the female name – acute accent. You could be forgiven for thinking that the list of manuscripts would be different to the list that had previously been cited in support of the masculine reading, but think again. Astonishingly, the list contains the same manuscripts. This means that between UBS3 and UBS4 the same manuscripts have been cited in support of both a masculine and a feminine reading!

As stated above, it is accepted that argument 5 is factually correct. NA26 does have a circumflex accent. However, it is also factually correct to state that the more up to date NA27 has an acute accent. And bringing matters right up to date, the current edition NA28 also has an acute accent which you can see for yourself by looking at the online edition here http://www.nestle-aland.com/en/read-na28-online/text/bibeltext/lesen/stelle/55/160001/169999/

Faced with the contradictions between NA26 and NA27 and UBS3 and UBS4, we have no choice but to put expert opinion to one side and put the evidence centre stage. There is after all a very easy way of resolving this issue; just look at the evidence, the manuscripts, and see for ourselves whether they have an acute accent or a circumflex accent.

The Internet age has brought many benefits, among which is the ability to provide access to manuscripts that were previously only accessible to a small number of academics. The original manuscripts are stored in various locations around the world, but thanks to modern technology digital photos or scans of those manuscripts can be viewed online. They are in fact fascinating historical manuscripts and contain beautifully and intricately written Greek text. There are various websites where different manuscripts can be viewed, but two of the best can be found at www.vmr.bham.ac.uk and www.csntm.org

As an aside I should point out that if you are unfamiliar with New Testament Greek and these types of manuscripts, finding the spot where the name Junia is written in Romans 16:7 can be like looking for a needle in a haystack. To save you the task I have done some of the work for you. Up to now you may have been wondering why you should believe my word over that of expert scholars of New Testament Greek. The picture on the next page should assist you.

It is a picture of a page from a manuscript, which dates to the 12th century. The original is located in Florence and the manuscript has been given the reference of GA620. Because it post-dates the 9th century it is written with accents, and all over the page you can see various accents written in the text. It will not surprise you to learn that this particular page is part of the book of Romans, and more particularly it includes verse 7 of chapter 16. For those of you who enjoy word search puzzles, I have not highlighted the verse. You will recall from chapter 5 that the name Junia in Greek looks like this – 'ιουνιαν'. To complete the puzzle all you have to do is find that word in the text in the picture and then see if it has an acute or circumflex accent.

Alternatively, if you are like me and have very little patience or inclination to do word searches, you can look on the next page where there is a close up picture of the relevant text with the word 'ιουνιαν' highlighted and the accent clearly visible.

GA620 – close up

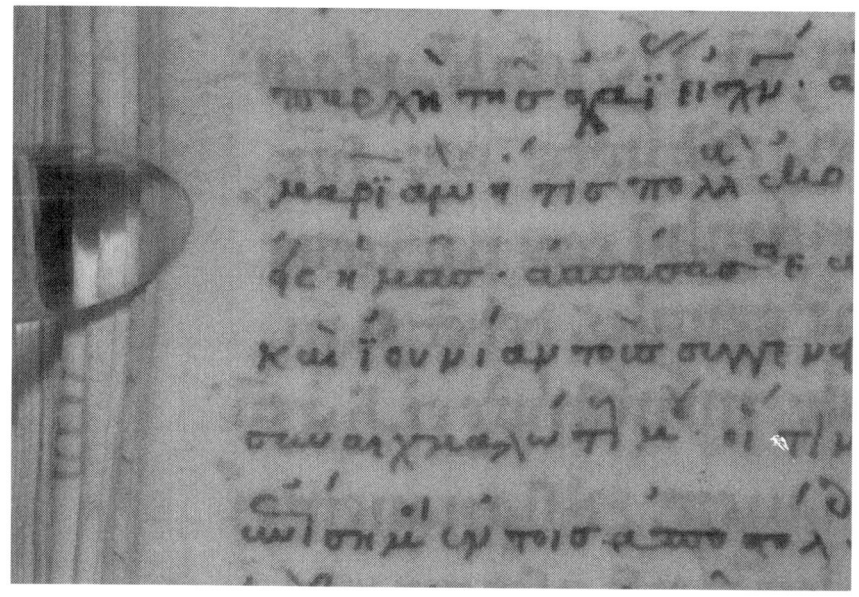

GA620 – close up with 'Junia' highlighted showing acute accent

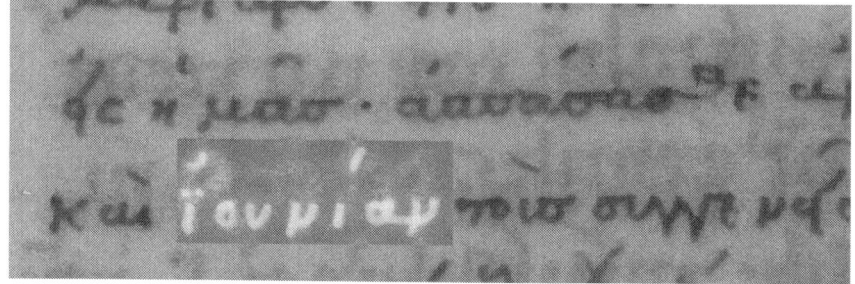

Just in case you might think this 12th century manuscript is the exception rather than the rule, here's another picture, and it's my personal favourite.

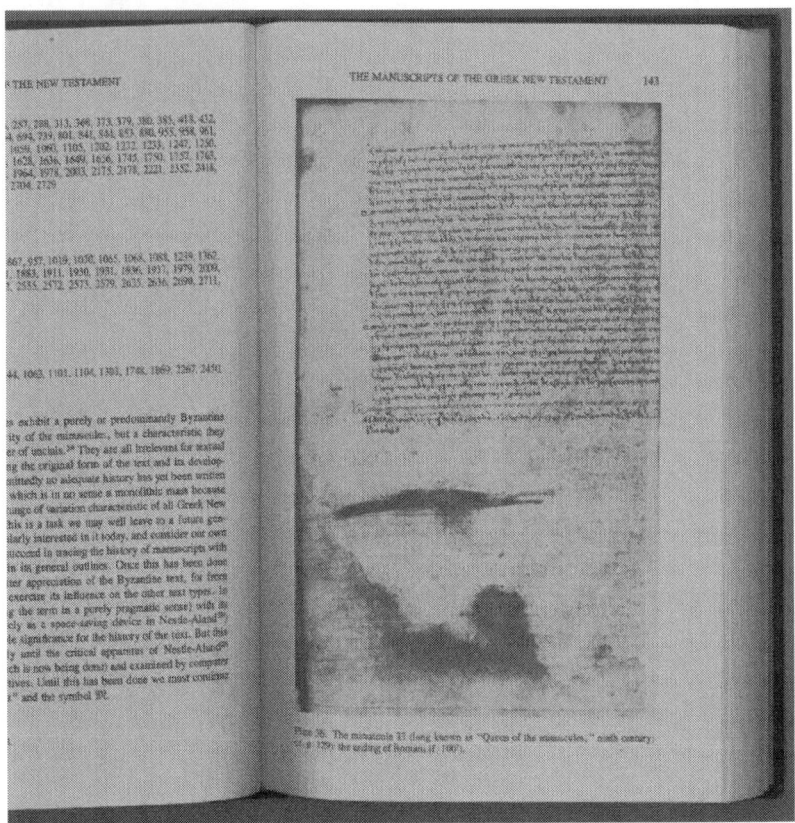

This is a picture of a page from a modern day book called 'The Text of the New Testament'. It is an excellent and informative book. On page 243, in a section where it is dealing with Greek manuscripts, it includes a picture of a minuscule called minuscule 33, or more commonly known as the 'Queen of minuscules'. It dates from the 9th or 10th century and as with GA620, it is written in Greek with accents.

The reason this picture is my favourite is because of all the pages of minuscule 33 which the author of the book could have shown, he chose the very page which contains verse 7 of Romans chapter 16! Again, for the benefit of word search aficionados I have not highlighted the word 'ιουνιαν', but at the end of this chapter I have reproduced a close up picture of the relevant text with the word 'ιουνιαν' highlighted. Again, the accent is plain for all to see.

Time and space does not allow me to show pictures of all the manuscripts with accents which contain Romans 16:7, so you'll either have to take me at my word or go and look for yourself. Put simply, the opposite of argument 10 is true. The fact is that all Greek manuscripts from the 9th century onwards accent the name as feminine. I am right and argument 10 is wrong because evidence always trumps expert opinion.

Conclusion

Argument 5 is correct, but as we've seen it doesn't help the cause of those who argue against Junia being a woman at all. Argument 10 is just plain and indisputably wrong.

The evidence is indecisive. Really? Only if indecisive means all the evidence totally and utterly points one way with not a shred of evidence pointing the other way!

CBMW
1. Older translations typically rendered the name in a masculine form;
2.
3.
4. The majority of modern translations favour the masculine;
5.
6.
7. It is the shortened form of the male name Junianus;
8.
9.
10.

66

RBMW
   11.
   12.
   13.
   14.
   15. It is a shortened form of a masculine name;
   16.

EFBT
   17.
   18.
   19.
   20. It could be a shortened form of a man's name.

Minuscule 33 – close up with 'Junia' highlighted showing acute accent

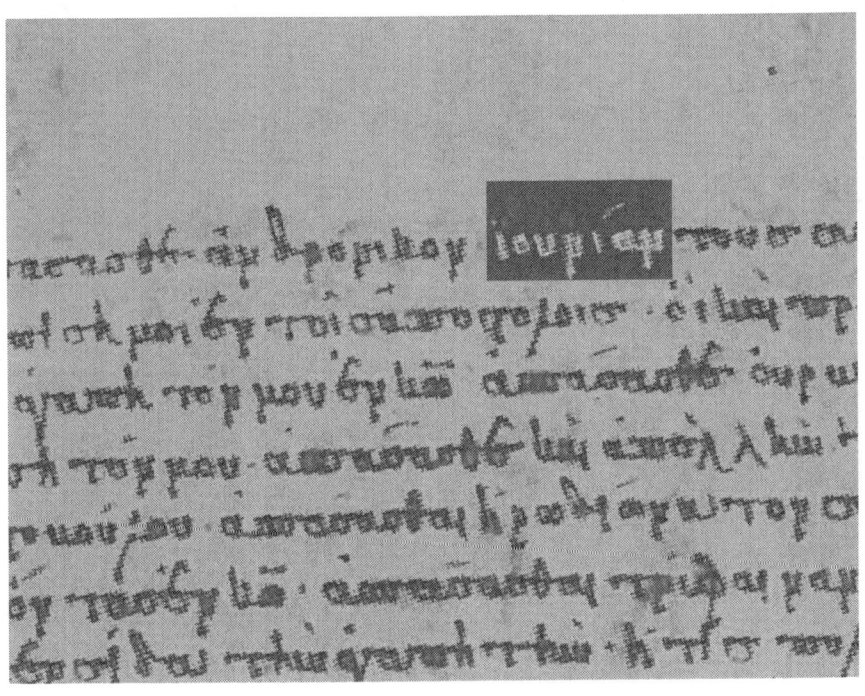

Chapter 10

Bible Translations

CBMW
1. **Older translations typically rendered the name in a masculine form;**
2.
3.
4. **The majority of modern translations favour the masculine;**
5.
6.
7. It is the shortened form of the male name Junianus;
8.
9.
10.

RBMW
11.
12.
13.
14.
15. It is a shortened form of a masculine name;
16.

EFBT
17.
18.
19.
20. It could be a shortened form of a man's name.

With a somewhat shrinking list of arguments we come to the subject of Bible translations. Here the arguments are straightforward and can be dealt with fairly quickly.

Argument 1

The first and obvious question that arises is what is meant by the word 'old'? Does it mean 50 years ago or 500 years ago? The argument does not say, but absent a reference point for what is defined as 'old' it is difficult if not impossible to prove or disprove the argument.

Doing the best we can, here is a list of English Bible translations that rendered the name in the masculine form – Junias. The list also shows the dates the various translations came out.

Dickinson 1837
Emphasised Bible (Rotherham) 1870''s-90's
Revised Version 1881
Rheims: American Edition 1899
American Standard Version 1901
Goodspeed 1902
Complete Bible (Fenton) 1903
Modern Reader's Bible 1907
Moffatt 1913
Ronald Knox 1945
Revised Standard Version 1946
Phillips 1947
Amplified New Testament 1958
New English Bible 1961
Noli 1961
Modern King James Version 1962
New American Standard Bible 1963
Jerusalem Bible 1966
Good News Bible 1966
Living Bible 1971
New International Version 1973
New Jerusalem Bible 1985
The Message 1993
Contemporary English Version 1995

It can be seen that the first in time on the list is the Dickinson Bible of 1837. The list includes the Revised Standard Version in 1946 and continues to the Modern King James Version. In total there are 24 translations on the list. I am not claiming it to be an exhaustive list and if you recall from chapter 4, you can compile your own modern day list by going to www.biblegateway.com.

Here is a list of English Bible translations that rendered the name in feminine form – Junia.

Tyndale 1525
Cranmer 1539
Great Bible (Cromwell) 1539
Geneva Bible 1560
Bishops Bible 1568
Rheims 1582 (Julia)
King James Version 1611
Variorum NT 1876
Weymouth 1903
Lamsa 1940
New American Bible 1970
New King James Version 1979
New Century Version 1987
New American Bible 1987
Revised English Bible 1989
New Revised Standard Version 1989
Oxford Inclusive Version 1995
New Living Translation 1996
English Standard Version 2001

It can be seen that the first in time on the list is Tyndale's Bible of 1525. In date order there are 7 translations before you get to the year 1837 when the first translation on the 'masculine form' list came out.

In total, there are 19 on the feminine form list and 24 on the masculine form list.

Of course, when you consider the history of the NA Greek text and the fact that most translations in the last 100 years used the NA text as their point of reference, it is not surprising that many translations in the last 100 years adopted the masculine form.

The underlying reason for many of the translations adopting the masculine form was the Greek text they were based on. It is also worth noting that people can get very caught up with arguments over translations and can hold them in very high esteem. I have heard it said to me, 'surely all the people on the translation committees cannot be wrong'. To which the short answer is, yes they can.

There is also an understandable habit of focusing only on English translations. However, English is not the only language the Bible has been translated into and it can often be informative to look at non-English translations. For present purposes one particularly relevant modern day language translation springs to mind. After all, if we are considering a word from 1st Century Greek, it will be very interesting to see how it is translated in modern day Greek. And I suspect by now it won't surprise you to learn that modern day Greek Bibles have the Junia of Romans 16:7 as a woman.

Conclusion

These arguments add nothing to the case against Junia being a woman.

CBMW
    1.
    2.
    3.
    4.
    5.
    6.
    7. It is the shortened form of the male name Junianus;
    8.
    9.
    10.

RBMW
    11.
    12.
    13.
    14.
    15. It is a shortened form of a masculine name;
    16.

EFBT
    17.
    18.
    19.
    20. It could be a shortened form of a man's name.

Chapter 11

Shortened name theory

<u>CBMW</u>
1.
2.
3.
4.
5.
6.
7. It is the shortened form of the male name Junianus;
8.
9.
10.

<u>RBMW</u>
11.
12.
13.
14.
15. It is a shortened form of a masculine name;
16.

<u>EFBT</u>
17.
18.
19.
20. It could be a shortened form of a man's name.

These arguments are all the same and are simply an assertion of what is known as the 'shortened name theory.' The theory goes that the name Junia is in fact a shortened version of the longer name Junianus. If you like, similar to 'Chris' being a shortened form of 'Christopher'. The technical name for the shortened form is a 'hypocorism'. There is no doubt that Junianus is a man's name, so the shortened version of Junia which appears in Romans 16:7 is also a man's name.

This has all the makings of an excellent argument in favour of Junia being a man. At least that is until we come to consider the evidence.

Evidence

The shortened name theory was first suggested in the 19th Century.

Before then there does not appear to be any record, in any language, of the theory having been put forward. The cynic might suggest that it is no coincidence that this theory appeared and grew in popularity around the same time as scholarly opinion was swinging away from Junia being a man due to the circumflex accent. After all, faced with a sinking ship when it came to Junia being a man, the only options were to accept a female apostle (to some a fate worse then death) or find a life raft. Fortunately, at just the right time, a life raft called the shortened name theory was discovered. Unfortunately, as we shall shortly see, it had a great big hole in the bottom.

All was not lost, however, as some were able to stay alive by clinging on to debris until a second life raft was discovered, this time called the 'known to the apostles' life raft. But as we shall see in chapters 13-23, that life raft is perhaps the most unseaworthy vessel ever to have taken to the high seas.

An obvious defect with the shortened name theory can be demonstrated by two personal examples. My dad's name is Ken. As with Chris and Christopher, Ken is not his full first name but everyone I know has always called him Ken. Everyone that is apart from my grandmother, his mother, who would always insist on calling him by the full name she had given him when he was born. If I am giving this example to an audience I always stop at this point to ask what they think my dad's full first name is and invariably the answer given is 'Kenneth'. Whilst that is a perfectly understandable answer, it is not the name on my dad's birth certificate. His full first name is in fact, 'Kenwyn'.

On the other hand, my wife is called Kate. Again, everyone we know calls her Kate. But on our Wedding Day when we said our vows we had to refer to her full first name of Katherine.

Everyone accepts that names can be shortened, but the point of these examples is to demonstrate that even with modern day names we cannot always be certain what a shortened name has been shortened from. And if we can't be certain with modern English names, we can be even less certain with Greek or Latin names from 2,000 years ago.

You may recall argument 17 which referred to Chris and Pat. That argument disappeared when it was shown there was in fact no evidence to support the contention that Junia had been a man's name. The same fate awaits arguments 7, 15 and 20 and for the same reason – a complete lack of evidence.

As we saw in chapter 7, there is not a single instance of the name Junias (man's name) appearing in Latin literature. Whenever the name Junia appears it is a woman's name. The Latin name Junianus does appear in Latin literature and it is a man's name. Accordingly, whilst the longer name Junianus does exist, there is not a shred of evidence to support the assertion that it was or could be shortened to the name Junias.

As if the complete lack of supporting evidence was not enough, there is another problem with the theory. As we have seen, longer names do get shortened and the technical term for the shortened name is a 'hypocorism'. However, when known (as opposed to theoretical) hypocorisms have been studied, a pattern has emerged as to how you get the shortened name from the longer version.

A good example is the longer Latin name Julianus. When this is shortened we find the name Julas. The important point to note is that the letter 'i' is dropped from the word when it is shortened. Accordingly, Julianus becomes Julas and not Julias. Explained another way, the last two letters 'as' are always added on after a consonant, not a vowel. Hence they are not added on to an 'i' (vowel), so the 'i' is dropped and they are added on to the 'l' = Julas.

Applying this to the longer name of Junianus, the shortened version would in fact be Junas. Thus, even if the longer name Junianus was shortened (which is only a theory in any event), it would not be shortened to Junias.

Unlike with Junianus, we do have actual evidence of a hypocorism in respect of a different longer Latin name. The name Julianus does appear in Latin literature, as does its shortened version, Julas. This is exactly what we would expect to find given the method of shortening names as described above.

Putting all this together we can summarise the position in respect of the shortened name theory as follows

1. The male Latin name Junianus does exist.
2. The male Latin name Junias does not exist.
3. Hypocorisms do exist.
4. Hypocorisms are formed by adding the letters 'as' to a consonant, not a vowel.
5. The male Latin name Julianus does exist.
6. The male Latin name Julas does exist.
7. There is no evidence of Junianus ever being shortened.
8. If Junianus was shortened, it would be to Junas, just as Julianus becomes Julas.

Conclusion

The shortened name theory is not supported by any evidence and what evidence there is contradicts the theory. Frankly, it is akin to me promoting a theory that Ken is a shortened name for Katherine. In support of my theory I rely on the fact that if you drop the second, third, fourth, sixth, seventh, and ninth letters from the long name you get the shortened name of Kate. There's no evidence to support my theory and what evidence there is in fact contradicts it, which puts it in exactly the same position as the shortened name theory for Junias.

In the absence of evidence it is easy to see why Egalitarians view those who promote this theory as people who are acting out of desperation, driven on by a predetermined view. On no account can they even contemplate the possibility that there was a female apostle, so faced with a choice between a female apostle and a really bad theory, they'll chose the really bad theory every time.

As many of you may have guessed some time ago, this leaves our list of arguments against Junia being a woman looking like this:

CBMW
    1.
    2.
    3.
    4.
    5.
    6.
    7.
    8.
    9.
    10.

RBMW
    11.
    12.
    13.
    14.
    15.
    16.

EFBT
    17.
    18.
    19.
    20.

All arguments against having failed to stand up to scrutiny, we have reached the point where we can say with certainly that the Junia spoken of in Romans 16:7 was a woman. It is interesting to note, however, that despite the overwhelming evidence set out above, some Complementarians, but not all, still maintain either that Junia was a man or that there is insufficient evidence to say she was a woman. This refusal to change their mind in the face of overwhelming evidence merely highlights the points I made in chapter 3. For some Complementarians the evidence is irrelevant. Their pre-determined position, based on 1 Timothy 2, is that a woman cannot be an apostle. Their interpretation of 1 Timothy 2 being non-negotiable, their options are limited.

Some choose to maintain Junia was not a man, and indeed this has been the choice of the majority for most of the last few hundred years. However, as the evidence has become more and more clear in favour of Junia being a woman, many Complementarians have realised that to deny Junia's womanhood is untenable. More untenable to them, however, would be acceptance of Junia as a woman apostle, so other objections to Junia's apostolic status had to be found.

To continue the sinking ship and life raft analogy, most Complementarians realise the ship called 'Junia was a man' has gone to a watery grave. Many are currently pinning their hopes of survival on a life raft called 'known to the apostles', but a few have opted instead to cling to some driftwood called 'apostle or messenger?' Before considering the seaworthiness of the life raft, we will first consider whether the driftwood has any buoyancy.

Chapter 12

Apostle or Messenger?

It is not enough to prove that Junia was a woman. My intention is to show not only that Junia was a woman, but that she was an apostle. In order to establish her apostolic status, I have to go beyond her gender and demonstrate that the word in Romans 16:7 is referring to 'apostles' as opposed to 'messengers'.

Thus we come to the second of our three main questions; were the people referred to in Romans 16:7 apostles?

I have already said why I believe people raise this argument; they raise it because it gives them a way out in case they lose the argument on Junia being a woman. Ironically, some of the evidence that causes them to lose that argument is the very same evidence that causes them to lose the argument between apostle and messenger.

The question of 'apostle or messenger?' is really a question as to how the Greek word 'αποστολοισ' 'apostolos' should be translated. The word appears in Romans 16:7 and is the last word in the group of words underlined below:

> Romans 16:7
> ασπασασθε ανδρονικον και **ιουνιαν** τουσ συγγενεισ
> μου και συναιχμαλωτουσ μου οιτινεσ εισιν **επισημοι**
> **εν τοισ αποστολοισ** οι και προ εμου γεγονασιν εν
> χριστω

Those who argue for the translation 'messenger' are quick to point out that the word 'apostolos' can be translated as 'messenger' as well as 'apostles'. The Liddell-Scott lexicon entry for 'apostolos' is as follows:

1. messenger, ambassador, envoy, he went off on a
mission to Laced., b. commander of a naval force,
2. messenger from God; esp. of the Apostles.

As the word can be and is translated elsewhere as 'messengers', the argument goes that that is how it should be translated in Romans 16:7, which in turn denies Junia any apostolic status.

<u>The case for Apostle</u>

The word 'messenger' appears on a number of occasions in the New Testament. Sometimes the Greek word that is translated into English as 'messenger' is *'angelos'*. Examples of these instances include Matt 11:10, Mark 1:2, Luke 7:24, Luke 7:27, Luke 9:52, 2 Cor 12:7 and James 2:25. Other times the Greek word is 'apostolos', such as in John 13:16. It must therefore be conceded that the word 'apostolos' can mean 'messenger' as well as 'apostle'.

When deciding the meaning of the word 'apostolos' in Romans 16:7, it is important to bear in mind that Romans was written by or on behalf of Paul. Accordingly, whilst the use and meaning of the word in the whole of the New Testament is informative, its use and meaning in books written by or on behalf of Paul will be even more informative.

There are only two occasions in all of the Pauline writings where he uses the word 'apostolos' to mean 'messenger.' These occur in 2 Corinthians 8:23 (*'messengers of the Churches'*) and Philippians 2:25 (*'your messenger'*).

There are many occasions where Paul uses the word 'apostolos' to mean apostle, as set out below in chronological order as the books appear in the New Testament.

Rom 1:1; Rom 1:5; Rom 11:13
1 Cor 1:1; 1 Cor 4:9; 1 Cor 9:1; 1 Cor 9:2; 1 Cor
9:3; 1 Cor 9:5; 1 Cor 12:28; 1 Cor 12:29; 1 Cor
15:7; 1 Cor 15:9
2 Cor 1:1; 2 Cor 11:13; 2 Cor 11:5; 2 Cor 12:11; 2
Cor 12:12
Gal 1:1; Gal 1:17; Gal 1:19; Gal 2:8
Eph 1:1; Eph 2:20; Eph 3:5; Eph 4:11
Col 1:1
1 Thess 2:6
1 Tim 1:1; 1 Tim 2:7
2 Tim 1:1; 2 Tim 1:11
Titus 1:1

I do not suggest that the argument is won by weight of numbers, but it is clear that on the vast majority of times when Paul used the word 'apostolos' he used it to mean 'apostles' as opposed to 'messengers'.

In addition to weight of numbers, however, there is another factor in favour of the meaning 'apostle'.

If you look again at the two instances where Paul used the word to mean 'messengers', you will see that on both occasions the word came with a qualifier attached. In 2 Corinthians 8:23 the qualifier is 'of the Churches' and in Philippians 2:25 it is 'your'. In the passage in Romans 16:7, however, there is no qualifier. Thus, if the word in Romans 16:7 were to mean 'messenger' it would be the only time Paul ever used the word in that way without a qualifier. The same cannot be said for the meaning 'apostle' as Paul frequently used the word to mean 'apostle' without any qualifier. Accordingly, Paul's use of the word in Romans 16:7 fits in with his use of the word elsewhere when he means 'apostle', but does not fit in with his use elsewhere when he means 'messenger'.

Some have questioned whether Paul could have been referring to an 'apostle' on the basis that only the Twelve were apostles, but I am not clear as to how they treat Paul, who was not one of the Twelve but who very clearly considered himself to be an apostle.

Not only did Paul consider himself to be an apostle, but in his writings he also clearly referred to Barnabus, the brothers of Jesus, Silvanus/Silas and Apollos as being apostles.

It is also clear that Paul considered the apostles to be more than or different than the Twelve. This can be seen in 1 Cor 15:5-9 where Paul tells us that the risen Christ was seen by Cephas, then the Twelve, then above 500, after that James, then *all the apostles*', then, last of all, by Paul.

This order also fits in with the information given to us in Romans 16:7 where we are told that Andronicus and Junia were not only Paul's *'kinsmen'* and *'fellow prisoners'*, but they were *'in Christ before Paul'*. It would therefore follow that they could be included in *'all the apostles'* who saw the risen Christ.

Church Fathers

If you cast your mind back to chapter 8 you will recall the details concerning the early Church Fathers, both Greek and Latin. Epiphanius aside, they spoke with one voice as to Junia being a woman. But Junia's gender was not the only thing on which they spoke with one voice. Tellingly, these Greek and Latin Church Fathers also considered that the person being spoken of in Romans 16:7 was an apostle. They did not think Junia was a messenger.

An oft repeated quote is that of Chrysostom:

> *'To be an apostle is something great but to be outstanding among the apostles, just think what a wonderful sum of praise that is. Indeed, how great the*

wisdom of this woman must have been that she was deemed worthy of the title of apostle.'

There can be no doubt from this quotation that Chrysostom considered Junia to be an apostle as opposed to a messenger.

We also saw in chapter 8 how many of the Latin Church Fathers discussed the probability or possibility that Junia was in the 70 that were sent out. Again, by discussing Junia being one of the 70, there can be no doubt that these Church Fathers considered Romans 16:7 to be speaking of apostles as opposed to messengers.

In fact, I have been unable to find a single reference in the first 1,000 years after Paul wrote Romans to any Church Father, Greek or Latin, asserting or even discussing the possibility that the person spoken of in Romans 16:7 was a messenger.

Bible Translators

In addition to the Church Fathers, the views of Bible translators are also informative. Again there is some irony here, as the reason many of the translators translated the name as a male name was because they were convinced the person being spoken of was an apostle, not a messenger. Those translators had a pre-determined view, which did not allow for a woman apostle. Had they thought the correct translation was messenger, they would have had no problem accepting Junia was a woman, but because they considered the correct translation to be 'apostle', they had to have Junia as a man.

If you've still got your list of translations for Romans 16:7 from www.biblegateway.com you will see that the vast majority of translations, irrespective of their view on whether Junia was a man or a woman, translate the word as 'apostles'.

Lexicons and Commentaries

The situation with lexicons and commentaries is also informative. Take, for example the lexicon by Gingrich and Danker. In discussing whether Junia was a man or a woman, the editorial committee said this:

> *'Some members, considering it unlikely that a woman would be among those styled apostles........'*

The point here is that the members of the committee were clearly of the view that the correct translation was 'apostles' as opposed to 'messengers'. It was because of this, together with their pre-determined view that women could not be apostles, that they opted for Junia being a man. Interestingly, they were prepared to change the gender of Junia but not prepared to change 'apostle' to 'messenger', which speaks volumes for their view as to the correct meaning of the word 'apostolos'.

The same point can be made in respect of Bauers. In commenting on Junia it states:

> *' .....possibility from a purely lexical point of view it is a woman's name...is probably ruled out by the context'.*

The only context this could be referring to is the fact that the person spoken of was an apostle. So again, the gender is changed because they considered the correct meaning of 'apostolos' to be apostle.

Another interesting passage is found in A Dictionary of the Bible by A.C. Headlam.

> *"There is little doubt as to whether the two are to be included among the apostles......in that case it is hardly likely that the name is feminine, although,*

> *curiously enough, Chrysostom does not consider the*
> *idea of a female apostle impossible."*

And again by Gingrich (1962)

> *"Grammatically it might be feminine, though this*
> *seems inherently less probable partly because the*
> *person is referred to as an apostle"*

And both J.B. Lightfoot and Lietzmann were of the view that Junia was a man because the person being spoken of was an apostle.

Conclusion

Just as with the man or woman question, the evidence in favour of 'apostle' as opposed to 'messenger' is overwhelming. Accordingly, having established that Junia was a woman and that the people being spoken of were apostles, all that now remains is to determine whether Junia was part of that group of apostles.

Chapter 13

An Apostle, or known to the Apostles?

We have arrived at the third and final question in respect of Junia; was she known *to* the apostles, or was she outstanding *among* the apostles? If it is the former, then despite the fact I have established Junia was a woman and that the people being referred to are apostles, I will have failed to demonstrate that Junia herself was an apostle. If it is the latter, however, then Junia will have been shown to be a female apostle.

From the last Chapter (and if you cast your mind back to Chapter 5) you will recall what Romans 16:7 looks like when written in Greek. Two parts of the passage were highlighted; the first being the name Junia and the second being the contentious phrase 'outstanding among/known to the apostles.' Just to refresh your memory, here it is again.

Romans 16:7

ασπασασθε ανδρονικον και **ιουνιαν** τουσ συγγενεισ

μου και συναιχμαλωτουσ μου οιτινεσ εισιν **επισημοι**

εν τοισ αποστολοισ οι και προ εμου γεγονασιν εν

χριστω

The question before us, therefore, is how should the phrase 'επισημοι εν τοισ αποστολοις' (episemoi en tois apostolos) be translated?

The overwhelming majority of English Bibles have translated this phrase in a way that denotes Junia as an apostle. The various readings include 'of note among the apostles' (KJV), 'outstanding among the apostles' (NIV), 'highly respected among the apostles' (NLT) and 'prominent among the apostles' (NRSV). As before, you can see all the various English translations at www.biblegateway.com/

There is a small minority of English Bibles, however, which translate the phrase in a way that denies Junia's apostleship.

If you look up Romans 16:7 in the ESV Bible you will see it reads as follows

> *'Greet Andronicus and Junia, my kinsmen and my fellow prisoners. They are well known to the apostles, and they were in Christ before me.'*

As an aside, the ESV has two footnotes in this verse. The first relates to the word Junia (with the footnote providing the alternative reading of 'Junias') and the second relates to the word apostle (with the footnote providing the alternative reading of 'messengers'). What is interesting, however, is that it does not have a footnote in respect of the phrase 'known to the apostles'. I can only take this to mean that the editors of the ESV are so confident in their view that there is no doubt whatsoever over this phrase, that unlike with the name 'Junias' and the word 'messenger', they consider the reader does not need to know of any alternative reading. Unfortunately, as the following chapters will show, the confidence of the editors of the ESV is very much misplaced and their failure to include even a footnote on this issue is a serious error of judgment.

Wayne Grudem is the senior editor of the ESV. On page 224 of EFBT he states:

> *"Prior to 2001, scholars had not done any significant computer-assisted research on the Greek construction (episemos + Dative) that is found in this verse, and therefore writings and translations before 2001 usually assumed that the meaning "well known among" was correct. But then in 2001, in an extensively researched technical article, the meaning "well known to" received strong support, with significant evidence from extrabiblical Greek. "'*

At the end of that quote is a footnote which confirms that the reference to the allegedly 'extensively researched technical article' is to a paper by M H Burer and D B Wallace.

If you look up Romans 16:7 in the NET you will see it reads as follows

> '*Greet Andronicus and Junia, my compatriots and my fellow prisoners. They are well known to the apostles, and they were in Christ before me.*'

As Grudem confirms at page 225 of EFBT, the same D B Wallace who co-authored the paper he refers to had '*significant influence*' over the NET Bible. It is perhaps not surprising therefore that the NET adopted the same reading which D B Wallace advocates in his paper.

There is a note in the NET Bible at Romans 16:7 which reads as follows:

> "*In collocation with words of perception, en plus dative personal nouns are often used to show the recipients*"'

So, both the ESV and the NET have adopted a translation which interprets the Greek phrase επισημοι εν τοισ αποστολοισ as meaning that Junia was well known *to* the apostles. And by being well known *to* the apostles as opposed to being outstanding *among* the apostles, Junia's apostleship is denied.

The question naturally arises as to why a small number of English Bibles have chosen to translate the phrase in this way.

To my knowledge, Grudem has cited no other paper or supporting evidence in support of the reading in the ESV. The NET does not cite any other paper. Accordingly, it would appear that the paper by Burer and Wallace is the sole basis for the translations of this phrase in both the ESV and the NET.

And this takes us into Robert Dick Wilson territory! We have returned to his quote on several occasions, but it will not hurt to consider it again in full.

> *"If a man is called an expert, the first thing to be done is to establish the fact that he is such; one expert may be worth more than a million other witnesses that are not experts. You will have observed that the critics of the Bible who go to it in order to find fault have a most singular way of claiming to themselves all knowledge and all virtue and all love of truth. One of their favourite phrases is, 'All scholars agree'. I wish to know who the scholars are and why they agree. Where do they get their evidence from to start with? My point is that you ought to be able to trace back this agreement amongst scholars to the original scholar who propounded the statement and then find out whether what that scholar said is true. What was the foundation of his statement?"*

Following this logic, it appears we have identified why the scholars [translators] agree. We have identified where they get their evidence from - the paper by Burer and Wallace. Wilson's point was correct. We have been able to trace back this agreement among scholars to the original scholar(s) who propounded the statement. Having done that, the final part of Wilson's statement now has to be addressed; '...*then find out whether what [Burer and Wallace] said is true. What was the foundation of [their] statement?*'

To a detailed examination of the Burer and Wallace paper we must now turn.

Chapter 14

Introduction to Burer and Wallace

The full title of the Burer and Wallace paper is *"Was Junia really an apostle? A re-examination of Romans 16 verse 7."* It was published in 2001 in New Testament Studies, a peer-reviewed academic journal published by Cambridge University Press. You can view a copy of the paper online here http://talmidimyeshua.org.docs/WasJuniaApostle.pdf or by typing 'Burer and Wallace Junia' into Google and then clicking on the first result in the list.

I am going to deal with the paper in three stages. First, I will set out a summary of the paper. Secondly, I will highlight some initial concerns. Thirdly, I will subject the paper to critical examination.

As it is essential to gain an understanding of what the paper is saying, we will need to delve into some more technical aspects of New Testament Greek. For those unfamiliar with New Testament Greek I would suggest that before you read the summary of the paper or the paper itself, you first refresh your mind by re-reading the section on New Testament Greek in Chapter 5.

As to the phrase in question, it will help to break it down into individual words.

επισημοι εν τοισ αποστολοισ

Below is each word in Greek, followed by the same word using English letters, followed by a slight variant in brackets. Underneath each word is either an extract from the definition given in the Liddell-Scott Greek lexicon (dictionary) or a link to the full definition. The online edition of Liddell-Scott can be found at http://stephanus.tlg.uci.edu/lsj/#eid=1&context=lsjb

As stated previously, when Greek words are cited in lexicons they always appear in the Nominative singular form. This is the 'slight variant' form referred to above which appears in brackets below.

επισημοι. = 'episemoi' (episemos)

distinguishing mark, device; badge, badge or *bearing* on a shield; *ensign* or *flag* (or *figurehead*) of a ship; *device* on a coin, on a signet; *serial number,*. II. generally, *mark, imprint.*

εν = 'en' (en)

See here for full definition
http://stephanus.tlg.uci.edu/lsj/#eid=35763&context=lsj&action=from-search

τοις = 'tois' (toi)
See here for full definition:
http://stephanus.tlg.uci.edu/lsj/#eid=107096&context=lsj&action=from-search

αποστολοις = apostolois (apostolos)

1. *messenger, ambassador, envoy,*. b. *commander of a naval force,* 2. *messenger from God,* esp. of the *Apostles.*

It can be seen from the above that the first word in the phrase is 'episemoi', or, in the Nominative singular, 'episemos'. These words appear time and time again in the Burer and Wallace paper and in my examination of it.

Chapter 15

Summary of Paper

The following is my summary of the main points as they appear on each page of the paper. It is provided to assist the reader in understanding the paper but should in no way be treated as a substitute for reading the paper itself. To obtain the best understanding I would recommend getting a copy of the paper and reading the first page, then returning here to read the summary of that page, and so on with each page of the paper.

As the paper appeared in the New Testament Journal, my copy of it has the page numbering from that journal, meaning the first page of the paper is paginated as page 76 of the journal. To avoid confusion the page references below start with the internal page number of the paper and are followed by the page number of the New Testament Journal. So, for example, page two of the paper is page 77 of the Journal, so is referred to as page 2/77. I have used the same method of page referencing in the critical examination in Chapter 19.

Page 1/76

Points out that there are normally two issues that are examined in respect of Junia; the first being whether she is a man or a woman and the second whether the Junia being spoken of is part of the apostolic band.

It is worth noting that the authors do not identify the issue of 'apostle or messenger' as a live issue.

The issue of Greek accents is referred to and the authors agree that the majority of Greek Fathers say Junia was a woman. Tellingly, they accept that the instance of Origen allegedly referring to Junia as a man is a translation mistake and that Origen did in fact refer to Junia as being a woman. I presume that unlike Grudem, they were able to find time to check this out for themselves.

92

Epiphanius is referred to as being the only Greek father during the 1,200 years immediately following Paul writing Romans who referred to Junia as a man. The authors do not mention whether Epiphanius understood the Greek of Romans 16:7 as meaning Junia was an apostle as opposed to being known to the apostles.

Page 3/78

The TLG is mentioned and they accept that the views of scholars over the last 20 years point to Junia being a woman – a view they agree with. Thus, the first issue in respect of whether Junia is a man or woman is treated as having been settled in favour of Junia being a woman.

There is, then, a passing reference to the 'technical sense' of the word apostle, as to whether it means apostle or messenger, but this point is not developed.

This takes the authors to the main point they wish to challenge and the purpose of their paper, the issue of 'well known *to* the apostles' or 'well known *among* the apostles.'

Page 4/79

The authors contend that scholarly discussion to date has only really concentrated on whether Junia was a man or a woman, with some secondary discussion about whether the word means apostle or messenger. As a result, say the authors, there has been little scholarly discussion about whether the Greek phrase should be translated as 'well known *to* the apostles' or 'well known *among* the apostles' and instead the latter translation has just been assumed. They consider this lack of discussion to be a flaw in the scholarly debate.

The difference between the competing translations is described as being 'inclusive' or 'exclusive'. 'Inclusive' is taken to mean that

Junia was included in the group being spoken of and would thus result in a translation of 'well known *among* the apostles.' 'Exclusive' means that Junia was excluded, or outside of the group, resulting in the translation 'well known *to* the apostles.'

So,   'among' = 'inclusive' = apostle
        'to' = 'exclusive' = not an apostle.

The authors accept that the vast majority of commentators adopt the 'inclusive' view. But they put this down to an assumption for which, they assert, there is no evidential support.

In adopting the terms 'inclusive' and 'exclusive' the authors tell us (footnote 13) they are taking their cue from a paper by Richard Cervin. We will consider the views of Richard Cervin in more detail when we subject the Burer and Wallace paper to critical examination.

Page 5/80

The modern scholarly position is traced back to Bishop Lightfoot and it is asserted that all modern scholars simply repeat and take as fact what Lightfoot said. It is suggested that because Lightfoot was and is held in such high esteem as a world-renowned Greek scholar, his view is accepted without question. However the authors assert that Lightfoot offered no evidence to support his view other than the views of the Greek Fathers.

Page 6/81

Because it is a minority view, it is suggested that those scholars who argue for the 'exclusive' meaning tend to supply more evidence to back up their position. However, the authors state that even then they do not fully address the grammatical evidence.

Page 7/82

Similar points are made in respect of the writings of those engaged in specialised studies on the role of women in the Church, in that it is asserted they simply assume the 'inclusive' meaning.

Page 8/83

Modern translations, it is said, tend to be 'inclusive' and only a handful of translations are 'exclusive'. They list three in the paper on page 9, the CEB, the Amplified and NET. (To this list we can add the ESV, which came out after Burer and Wallace published their paper). And they say in the last three decades, the 'exclusive' view has only scarcely been attested in translations or in theological literature. So they are very much putting forward a theory that is in the absolute minority, but they assert that the arguments against their view, the 'exclusive' view, are largely a snowballing dogma that has little substance at its core.

Page 9/84

Now they come to the evidence that Junia was not an apostle and they set out their thesis: The Greek phrase in Romans 16:7 is more naturally interpreted as 'exclusive', 'known *to* the apostles', and not 'inclusive', 'well known *among* the apostles'. The remainder of the paper sets out to prove the thesis.

The first category of evidence they turn to is described as the lexical and syntactical evidence. Lexical is just another word for dictionary, so they are basically saying that Greek dictionaries support their thesis. As for syntactical, it's just a technical way of describing the grammatical arrangements of words in the sentences of a language. In short, it involves looking at the words in the context of the sentences and how they are used in normal usage.

The authors' claim is that when you look at the usage of the relevant words in Greek literature, it supports the 'exclusive' interpretation as being the preferred and usual reading.

Dealing first with lexicons, they say the word 'episemos' can mean 'well known, prominent, outstanding, famous, notable, or notorious'. They say the lexical stream can be broken into two streams; one is an implied comparative sense, 'prominent, outstanding among', and the second is in an elative sense.

Now there is a switching of words here, which can be a bit confusing. For the avoidance of doubt, when they say 'comparative' they mean 'inclusive' and when they say 'elative' they mean 'exclusive'.

Inclusive = comparative = apostle
Exclusive = elative = not an apostle

So, the translation 'well known *to*' would represent the elative/exclusive sense, whereas 'well known *among*' would represent the comparative/inclusive sense.

Turning to the syntactical evidence, they set out a working hypothesis, namely that if a noun in the Genitive is typically used with comparative adjectives, 'we might expect the same with an implied comparative'. Thus, if Romans 16:7 is an implied comparison (inclusive) 'we might expect Paul to use the Genitive; if it is elative (exclusive), we might expect 'εν' plus the Dative.'

All of that is starting to sound a little bit technical! But don't worry, it's not as complicated as it sounds.

Chapter 16

New Testament Greek revisited

At this point I need to take a diversion from the summary in order to consider some aspects of New Testament Greek.

You will recall that in Chapter 5 we looked at English grammar and words that were the object and the subject in a sentence. In Greek these words are said to be in the Nominative case (object) and Accusative case (subject). We can tell the case of a Greek word by looking at its ending; hence we know that the name Junia in Romans 16:7 is written in the Accusative case.

In Chapter 5 we only considered two cases; Nominative and Accusative. In order properly to understand the Burer and Wallace paper we now need to consider two more; Genitive and Dative.

It will assist by considering again the table setting out Greek words with their various endings.

Declension	2	1		2
Nominative singular	Λόγος	γραφή	ωρα	ἐργον
Genitive singular	Λόγου	γραφης	ωρας	ἐργου
Dative singular	Λόγω	γραφη	ωρα	ἐργω
Accusative singular	Λόγον	γραφήν	ωραν	ἐργον
Nominative plural	Λόγοι	γραφαι		ἐργα
Genitive plural	Λόγων	γραφων		ἐργων
Dative plural	Λόγοις	γραφαις		ἐργοις
Accusative plural	Λόγους	γραφας		ἐργα

Although it sounds technical, what Burer and Wallace are saying is in fact quite simple.

They start by referring to a comparative noun. I had hoped to get to the end of this book without resorting to quoting from Wikipedia, but alas, when it comes to explaining what is meant by a comparative noun I can do no better than quote the relevant Wikipedia entry:

> *"In linguistics, the **comparative** is a syntactic construction that serves to express a comparison between two (or more) entities or groups of entities in quality, quantity, or degree; it is one of the degrees of comparison, alongside the positive and the superlative. The comparative is signaled in English by the suffix -er or by a word of comparison (as, more, less) and the conjunction- or preposition-like word as or than. The comparative is frequently associated with adjectives and adverbs because these words take the -er suffix or modifying word more or less (e.g. faster, more intelligent, less wasteful); it can also, however, appear when no adjective or adverb is present, for instance with nouns (e.g. more men than women)."*

They state that in Greek, the Genitive case is typically used with a comparative noun. They then state that 'episemos' is an 'implied comparative' noun. They hypothesise that what is true of a comparative noun will also be true of an implied comparative noun, namely that the Genitive case will typically be used.

So, point one is that the first word in the phrase – 'episemos' – is an implied comparative noun.

The question Burer and Wallace then raise is; how should the word 'episemos' be translated?

Their answer is that it depends on what comes after it. In short, they assert that if what comes after it is in the Genitive Case, then 'episemos' should be translated in the 'inclusive' sense. However, if what comes after it is in the Dative Case, then 'episemos' should be translated in the 'exclusive' sense.

Put another way, they assert that if Paul, when writing Romans, had meant to say that Junia was an apostle, he would have used the Genitive Case after the word 'episemos', but if he had meant to say she was known *to* the apostles (i.e. not an apostle herself) then he would have used the Dative case after the word 'episemos'.

That is their hypothesis. Whenever you see 'episemos' followed by the Genitive it will be 'inclusive', whenever you see it followed by the Dative it will be 'exclusive'. This means that throughout their paper certain words are interchangeable and mean the same thing

Inclusive = comparative = Genitive = apostle
Exclusive = elative = Dative = not an apostle

This of course takes us to the phrase in Romans 16:7 where, as you may have guessed, the word 'episemos' is followed by the Dative. So, according to Burer and Wallace's hypothesis, the meaning of 'episemos' in Romans 16:7 is elative = 'exclusive'. And that is why the ESV says 'known *to* the apostles'.

This point can be seen in the quotation above from Grudem in EFBT. In arguing for the translation 'well known *to*' he refers to research on the 'Greek construction (episemos + dative)'. Although not obvious to the non-Greek speaking reader, he is referring to this disputed phrase in Romans 16:7 and the fact that in that verse the word 'episemos' is followed by the Dative case.

So, at risk of repetition, the paper from Burer and Wallace is basically saying that how you translate the word 'episemos' depends on what follows it. If it is followed by the Dative, it is NOT comparing, if it is followed by the Genitive, it IS comparing.

Thus

(Episemos + Dative) = inclusive = comparative = apostle
(Episemos + Genitive) = exclusive = elative = not an apostle

That is Burer and Wallace's thesis. Clearly, if they are right, Junia was not an apostle. So the obvious question arises; does the evidence support their thesis? Naturally, Burer and Wallace think it does and to see why we will have to return to the summary of their paper.

Chapter 17

Summary cont'd

Page 10/85

Having set out their thesis, Burer and Wallace turn to considering the evidence. Obviously, given the nature of their thesis, the evidence will need to involve instances in Greek literature where the word 'episemos' appears and where it is followed either by the Dative or Genitive Case. Those instances can then be examined to see if they show a clear pattern that whenever 'episemos' is followed by the Genitive it is 'inclusive' and whenever it is followed by the Dative it is 'exclusive'.

Before examining the evidence, Burer and Wallace explain what they consider to be relevant evidence. They say that we must compare apples with apples. In other words, the instances in Greek literature where the word 'episemos' appears are only relevant if they reflect the same sentence structure as the instance in Romans 16:7.

In this respect they say the 'substantival adjunct (i.e. either the noun in the Genitive or the object of the preposition 'en') should be personal.' What does that mean? It means that the noun in Romans 16:7 is the word 'apostles'. As this noun is talking about people, it is a personal noun, whereas a noun like the word 'chair' is not talking about people so is an impersonal noun.

So, to compare apples with apples, we are told we must look at examples where the word 'episemos' appears with a personal noun.

However, due to what the authors describe as the 'paucity of data', they say they will look at examples with impersonal nouns as well. In other words, because they weren't able to find that many examples containing personal nouns, they had to include examples with impersonal nouns.

Page 11/86

The authors now explain how they found the evidence they refer to in the paper. They explain that a computer search was carried out for the word 'episemos'. This came up with several hundred pages of text. In order to narrow the results the search terms were amended so that it only searched for two identifiable patterns, namely 1) episemos plus the Dative; and 2) episemos plus the Genitive. This caused the several hundred pages of text to be reduced to what they describe as 'a few dozen passages containing illuminating information and definite patterns.'

Having identified 'a few dozen passages' the authors proceed to divide them into five categories.

1. Biblical and patristic Greek
2. Papyri
3. Inscriptions
4. Literary texts
5. Hellenistic texts

The categories are merely describing where the passages were found. If they were found in biblical and patristic writings they went into that category, if on inscriptions into that category, and so on.

Biblical and Patristic Greek

Dealing first with Biblical and patristic Greek they say that whenever the phrase is comparative and 'inclusive' it is usually, if not frequently 'episemos' plus the Genitive case. That obviously supports their theory. When the phrase is elative and exclusive, 'en' plus a personal plural Dative is not uncommon. That supports their theory.

They sum up Biblical and patristic by saying that whilst the 'inclusive' reading is aided in some examples with impersonal noun plus a Dative, 'every instance' of personal inclusiveness uses Genitive not Dative.

Page 12/87

Papyri

They say the Papyri can be dispensed with relatively quickly as there are only a few examples. Four texts are cited, all of which are said to be 'inclusive' and all four use the Genitive. This supports their theory.

Page 13/88

Inscriptions

Turning to the Inscriptions category, they say the examples are not plentiful but do represent excellent parallels to the phrase in Romans 16:7. The authors state that the examples all point in one direction, namely that 'episemos' followed by 'en' plus personal Dative (as in Romans 16:7) is 'exclusive', not 'inclusive'.

Literary text

The evidence from literary texts is stated as being 'not quite so uniform'. Nevertheless, the authors state that the pattern that has emerged from the evidence thus far is still generally maintained. In this category there is only one example.

Page 14 /89

Hellenistic texts

The Hellenistic texts are described as being a bit more varied in their nuances. One example in this category is said to be 'the first parallel to Romans 16:7....that could offer real comfort to the inclusivists. It is unmistakable, it is personal, it is rare.' In other words, there is one example where 'episemos' is followed by the Dative and where the meaning is 'inclusive'.

Page 15/90

Having examined all the evidence they set out their conclusion. They say their study has produced surprising results and goes against the scholarly consensus. Repeatedly, their working hypothesis was borne out; whenever an 'inclusive' meaning was intended it was consistently episemos plus the Genitive Case and episemos plus the Dative case was almost never so used. Thus, they conclude, it is more accurate to say Romans 16:7 almost certainly means 'well-known *to* the apostles'

Page 16/91

The authors finish on the final page by observing that there is a broader implication to their study. They state that one has to wonder how there should be such a great chasm between scholarly opinions and what the data actually reveals.

Chapter 18

Initial Concerns

I have to say that upon reading the paper there were a number of matters that caused me concern. In other words, without reading the paper in a critical way and without exploring matters in any detail, certain statements in the paper caused alarm bells to ring in my mind. In and of themselves these issues do not mean that the paper is wrong, but they raise sufficient concern to make one want to look into matters in more detail and with a critical eye.

On the first page of the paper the authors state that there is quite a bit of evidence on both sides. This is in the context of the question of whether the name Junia is a man's or a woman's name. For reasons that should by now be pretty obvious, I do not accept for one second that there is quite a bit of evidence on both sides. I think there is no evidence on one side and overwhelming evidence on the other. Accordingly, the assertion that there was quite a bit of evidence on both sides caused me to raise my eyebrows.

Then the authors continue by saying that 'most commentators simply assume'. My immediate response to that assertion was: how do they know? They can't possibly know what was in the commentators' minds when they wrote what they wrote, so at best they are guilty of the same offence they lay at the commentators' doors – a bare assumption. They simply assume that the commentators assumed.

Then on page 3, you get footnote 12.

> *"We have already noted that the patristic authors are preoccupied with whether [Junia] is male or female, giving little substantive attention to what Paul has to say about this individual's relation to the apostolic band. That they seem to assume a particular view, without interacting over the force of the Greek, is hardly a sufficient reason to adopt their view, as Lightfoot, Fitzmyer, et al. have done"*

And I thought, hmm, so what you are telling me is, patristic authors (early Church Fathers) whose first language was Greek, writing a few hundred years after Paul wrote Romans, interpreted the phrase to be inclusive, i.e. they considered Junia to be an apostle. However, Burer and Wallace are asserting that because the patristic authors do not expressly state that they have considered whether the phrase is inclusive or exclusive, the patristic authors have not really considered the arguments and therefore their opinions should be ignored.

A hypothetical example from English will demonstrate my point. I have in front of me a copy of a book by Charles Darwin popularly known as 'Origin of the species', a shortened version of its full title *'On the Origin of Species by Means of Natural Selection, or the Preservation of Favoured Races in the Struggle for Life.'* It was first published in 1859. In Chapter Twelve Darwin deals with the subject of geographical distribution, where he discusses collecting species in Brazil. Specifically he refers to 'the freshwaters of Brazil'. As it happens I am in the process of writing a detailed review of that book and I am currently dealing with the issue of geographical distribution. In my review I have discussed the features of some freshwater species and mused over what influence if any the lack of salt in freshwater has had on the evolution of those species. I have written this because English is my first language, I am writing in English, to English speakers, and I know that in English the word 'freshwater' is referring to water that is not salty. As I know this is universally agreed by all educated English speakers I do not for one second consider there to be any need to include in my review an explanation as to why I consider the word 'freshwater' means water that it not salty. It just does.

Now fast forward nearly two thousand years to the year 4,000 AD. It turns out two academics, for whom English is not their first language, have come up with a theory that in 19th Century English the word 'freshwater' in Darwin's 'Origin of the Species' did not mean water that is not salty. In opposition to their theory another academic produces a copy of my review. He says my review is strong evidence against their theory because it was written in the 21st Century, less than 200 years after Charles Darwin wrote 'Origin of the Species'. He points out that English was my first language and that it is clear from my review that I understood the word 'freshwater' to mean water that is not salty.

Imagine that academic's surprise when the other two academics tell him my review is irrelevant and does not count as evidence. When pressed as to why this is so, they respond by saying that because I did not expressly state in my review why I considered the word 'freshwater' to mean water that is not salty, it is clear I did not really consider the arguments about what it meant and my opinion should therefore be ignored.

I trust it is obvious that my hypothetical example is as far fetched as Burer and Wallace's approach to evidence is absurd.

Next, on page 10/85 they talk about comparing apples with apples. In the context of their paper they explain this to mean comparing personal nouns with personal nouns and not with any impersonal nouns. It may be that this is a perfectly proper requirement, but as a reader of the paper I am left simply having to assume or accept that this is the case, as no reason is given by the authors. There is no explanation anywhere in the paper as to why the Greek meaning would be different for a personal noun than an impersonal noun.

If the authors, as they do, seek to assert that phrases with personal nouns should carry more evidential weight than those with impersonal nouns, then it is beholden on them to explain why. I want to know whether there is any grammatical reason for differentiating between personal and impersonal nouns when it comes to how they might affect the meaning of the word 'episemos'. If they are unable to produce evidence that shows a reason for differentiating, then I can see no basis for giving different evidential weight to examples with personal nouns.

I am not saying that the authors are wrong to differentiate between personal and impersonal nouns but I am saying that they ought to provide cogent reasons for doing so. Particularly when within their paper they dismiss an example that goes against their theory, purely on the basis it contains an impersonal as opposed to a personal noun.

Moving on to page 11, they say they manually narrowed the search, reducing the results from hundreds of pages to a few dozen texts. What is of concern is that nowhere do they give a proper explanation for the terms of the original search or the terms used for narrowing the search. Instead they use phrases such as 'examined further for their relevance' but without properly defining what they considered to be relevant.

In my view it is a serious error when the authors fail to disclose the actual data. They said they were left with a few dozen passages. Am I to assume this means 36? Upon closer examination I find that only 30 passages are refereed to in the paper, including in the footnotes. This either means 'a few dozen' meant 30 (which is not a few dozen), or there are 6 passages which are not discussed in the paper and which no one can examine for themselves because the authors have not disclosed all the data.

I'm afraid this is loose language and poor scholarship. The exact number of relevant passages should have been stated and somewhere in the paper, or in an appendix, a full list of those passages should have been provided.

This loose language continues elsewhere in the paper. The authors use words such as 'frequently' and 'uncommon' without defining exactly what they mean. When dealing with limited data (maximum of 36 passages) the authors should use precise figures, not vague words. For example, if 25% of the passages were said to support an inclusive meaning, would 9 out of 36 count as 'uncommon'? Would anything over 50% count as frequently?

On page 12 we see the phrase 'in every instance'. But what does this mean? Is it referring to 36 instances or 3 instances? If the former, every instance would appear to be strong evidence. If the latter, is it that persuasive?

At footnote 45 the authors tell us they owe a profound debt of gratitude to 'Chris Bradley of Princeton University who spent much of the summer of 1999 gathering the data, isolating the relevant constructions, translating many of the texts and offering his preliminary assessment of their value'.

A number of questions arise; who is Chris Bradley? What are his qualifications? On what basis did he isolate the relevant constructions? Of particular note is their statement that this Chris Bradley translated many of the texts. The reason this is important is because, as you will see in subsequent chapters, the accuracy of the translations of some of these texts is hotly disputed.

Two other footnotes cause concern. There's footnote 63 on page 14 which they don't discuss in the paper but which at first glance looks like it could be relevant evidence. The same applies for footnote 65 on page 15.

As to the use of footnotes generally, it is interesting to note that some of the data are referenced and dealt with in the main text whereas other data are consigned to the footnotes. Unfortunately no explanation is given as to the criteria applied in determining which data should go where. Absent an explanation, the cynic might conclude that data that didn't support the authors' theory were hidden away in the footnotes.

All of these concerns are in the context of a paper which is setting out to disprove a position which by the authors' own admission has been widely held and accepted by scholars the world over. If this paper is going to succeed in challenging scholarly opinion, it is almost certainly going to have to demonstrate the very highest standards of scholarship, which even a cursory examination of this paper shows it has failed to do. Put simply, one is left with the strong suspicion that this paper is not all it appears to be. The only way to be certain is to subject it to critical examination.

Chapter 19

Critical examination

A simple search of the Internet reveals that the authors of this paper are no mere laymen. Taking just one of them, D B Wallace has taught graduate level courses in New Testament Greek since 1979. He has a PhD from a Theological Seminary and is currently a professor of New Testament studies. Professor Wallace has written a Greek grammar, which has become a standard textbook in colleges and seminaries. In addition, he is the senior New Testament editor of the NET Bible and the executive director for the Centre for the study of New Testament Manuscripts.

Such an impressive CV works both ways. Clearly it suggests that Professor Wallace knows his Greek and that his opinions deserve to be treated seriously and with respect. However, it also means that we are entitled to expect and demand certain standards from Professor Wallace, which might not be demanded or expected of a lesser luminary.

Unfortunately, as will become clear, the paper comes nowhere near to meeting the standards expected of it. Putting it bluntly, Burer and Wallace's work is far from 'scholarly', their methods are highly questionable and they play fast and loose with the evidence. Further, in certain aspects their treatment of the Greek can best be described as incompetent.

As explained in the summary of the paper, Burer and Wallace base their case on 6 categories of evidence:

1. Lexical and Syntactical
2. Biblical and patristic Greek
3. Papyri
4. Inscriptions
5. Literary texts
6. Hellenistic texts

It is into these categories that the evidence – 'a few dozen passages' – falls. Burer and Wallace's conclusion is based on their assessment of the evidence. This point cannot be stressed too strongly. It is all too easy to focus on Greek words and to be impressed with other people's qualifications and ability to understand New Testament Greek. Let me be clear, qualifications and ability should not be ignored or undervalued, but they must not be allowed to distract our focus from the real issue at hand. If any meaningful critical examination of this paper is to take place one fundamental principle has to be established from the very outset. The matter at hand is one of Evidence.

Granted, an understanding of New Testament Greek is necessary to understand and evaluate some of the evidence, but the argument is not won by an appeal to who is best at New Testament Greek. We have before us a theory. In support of that theory the authors put forward 30 pieces of evidence (in addition to the lexical and syntactical argument). They assert that upon examination, those 30 pieces of evidence support their conclusion that it is more accurate to say Romans 16:7 almost certainly means 'well-known *to* the apostles'. Of course, it wouldn't be the first time in history that someone has allowed thirty pieces of something to affect their judgment.

Notwithstanding everything I have said about evidence, I am acutely aware that some of you may not be fully convinced that you or I have the ability or expertise to argue against people of the academic stature of Burer and Wallace. To address that concern I would like to introduce you to a man called Richard Cervin.

The more alert reader may remember that name from chapter 15. You may recall that he was the subject of footnote 13 in the Burer and Wallace paper and that Burer and Wallace said they were taking their cue from him by using the terms 'inclusive' and 'exclusive'. Professor Cervin has a PhD from the University of Illinois, an MA from the University of Illinois, and a BA from California State University, Fullerton.

It is extremely important to note that unlike Professor Wallace, who is a theologian, Professor Cervin is a linguist. His expertise is linguistics and his particular area of linguistic expertise is ancient Greek, i.e. the period for all the Greek referred to in Burer and Wallace's paper.

In preparing this critical examination I was fortunate enough to be able to enter into correspondence with Professor Cervin and to obtain his views on Burer and Wallace's paper. I was even more fortunate (and grateful) to obtain Professor Cervin's permission for me to quote from his correspondence with me. Accordingly, throughout this critical examination I have included extensive quotations from Professor Cervin, some of which may be more appropriate for those with an interest in the more technical arguments.

I am comforted by the fact that, as will be seen from his comments, expert linguistic opinion in the form of Professor Cervin is on my side, but I remain adamant that evidence trumps opinion. We can therefore countenance no further delay and to the Evidence we must now turn.

Lexical and Syntactical

As with the summary of the paper, keeping a copy of the paper to hand throughout our critical examination will assist the reader. Insofar as the issue at hand is concerned we can ignore the first few pages of the paper. For us, the issue begins half way down page 9/84 under the subheading 'Evidence that Junia was not an apostle'.

The assertion under this category is quite straightforward. Burer and Wallace state:

> "The lexical domain can roughly be broken down into two streams: episemos is used either in an implied comparative sense ('prominent, outstanding [among]') or in an elative sense ('famous, well known [to/by]')."

Unfortunately for them the Evidence paints a somewhat different picture.

Three exhibits are put before you, being the three lexicons referred to by Burer and Wallace.

1. LSJ

    The full title of this lexicon is Liddell-Scott-Jones Greek-English Lexicon and the online version can be found here:
    http://www.tlg.uci.edu/lsj/#eid=1&context=lsj

2. BAGD

    The Full title of this lexicon is the '*Greek-English Lexicon of the New Testament and Other Early Christian Literature*'. The name 'BAGD' comes from the surnames of the contributors, Bauer, Arndt, Gingrich & Danker. In fact, at about the same time as the Burer and Wallace paper came out, a new version of this lexicon was published and the name was changed to 'BDAG.' The four contributors were the same, just listed in a different order.

3. L&N

    The full title of this lexicon is the 'Greek-English Lexicon by Semantic Domains' and its name is taken from its authors, Johannes Louw and Eugene Nida. Also known as the 'Louw & Nida'

Let us examine each in turn.

Liddell Scott Jones

Here is the full entry in LSJ for the word 'episemos'

> *Ἐπί-σημος, Dor. ἐπί-σᾱμος, ον, (σῆμα) serving to distinguish, τοῖς δ' ὄνομ' ἄνθρωποι κατέθεντ' ἐ. ἑκάστῳ Parm. 19.3.*

II. having a mark, inscription or device on it, esp. of money, stamped, coined, χρυσὸς ἐ, opp. ἄσημος, Hdt.9.41; ἀργύριον Th.2.13; χρυσίον X.Cyr.4.5.40, cf.IG12.301, al.; so ἀναθήματα οὐκ ἐ. offerings with no inscription on them, Hdt.1.51; ἀσπίδες ἐ., opp. λεῖαι, IG12.280, cf. Men.526.

2. of epileptic patients, bearing the marks of the disease, Hp.Morb.Sacr.8; of cattle, spotted or striped, LXX Ge.30.42.

3. notable, remarkable, μνῆμ' ἐ. a speaking remembrance, S.Ant.1258 (anap.); ξυμφοραί E.Or.543; εὐνή, λέχος, Id.HF68, Or.21; τύχη Id.Med.544; χαρακτήρ Id.Hec.379; τάφος ἐπισημότατος Th.2.43; τιμωρία Lycurg.129; τόποι IG12(3).326.42 (Thera, Sup.); of garments, fine, SIG695.39 (Magn. Mae., ii B.C.); and of persons, ἐ. σοφίην notable for wisdom, Hdt.2.20; ἐ. ἐν βροτοῖς E.Hipp.103; ἐ. ξένοι Ar.Fr.543: in bad sense, conspicuous, notorious, ἐς τὸν ψόγον E.Or.249; δέσμιος ἐ. Ev.Matt.27.16; διὰ δημοκοπίαν Plu.Fab.14; ἐπὶ τῇ μοχθηρίᾳ Luc.Rh.Pr.25.

4. significant, οὐκ ἐ. Artem.1.59, 3.32.

III. Adv. ἐπισή-μως Plb.6.39.9, Sm.Ps.73(74).4, J.BJ6.1.8: Comp. -ότερον Gal.9.762; -οτέρως Artem.2.9: Sup. -ότατα Luc.Hist.Conscr.43.

Whilst the point may not immediately be obvious, on careful examination it can be seen that nowhere in this entry does LSJ include 'known to' as a possible meaning.

I am grateful to Professor Cervin for bringing to my attention the revised supplement to LSJ which came out in 1996 but which is not referred to by Burer and Wallace. On page 129 of the *Supplement,* there are notes on the entry for 'episemos' and they include the addition of a fifth definition, namely '*conspicuous*'. It is of course quite possible that 'conspicuous' (not in a bad sense) could be applicable in Rom. 16:7.

BDAG

Here is the abbreviated entry in BDAG

> - *splendid, prominent, outstanding, notorious*

The point will hopefully now be more obvious. Once again it can be seen that nowhere in this entry does BDAG include 'known to' as a possible meaning. However, in respect of the meanings it does include it cites the passage in Romans 16:7, the very passage we are considering, as evidence of the meaning 'prominent, outstanding'. Lest the irony of this be missed, this means that one of the lexicons Burer and Wallace plead in support of their case for translating the phrase in Romans 16:7 as 'known to', cites that exact same passage in support of the meaning 'prominent, outstanding [among]'.

Pausing there, this means that the two most well known and respected Greek Lexicons do not give 'known to' as a possible meaning for 'episemos'.

Louw & Nida

Here is the entry in L&N

> *28.31 Know (28) Well Known, Clearly Shown, Revealed (28.28-28.56) pertaining to being well known or outstanding, either because of positive or negative characteristics - outstanding, famous, notorious, infamous.*

116

Here we have, for the first time, a lexicon, which does include 'known to' as a possible meaning for 'episemos'. This means that Burer and Wallace's case is only supported by one out of three lexicons, with the one in support being the least well known and least used of the three Greek lexicons.

And at this point it is interesting to note what Professor Cervin has to say about the Louw & Nida lexicon:

> 'The problem with Louw & Nida is essentially philosophical (in terms of linguistics), which I personally would not expect theologians to understand. First, the lexicon purports to be based on "semantic domains" but the rather hidden issue is "Who decides on what those semantic domains are and why?" Semantic domains is a very subjective area and furthermore, domains themselves are often language specific. Concepts which native English speakers may naturally link together (as a domain) may seem silly, stupid, or downright insane to speakers of other languages, and vice versa; a Greek semantic domain may contain concepts that English speakers simply can't figure out how to put together (e.g. the word χαλός entails both the notions of "beauty" and of "goodness", but English speakers keep these two ideas separate).
>
> For example, the English word head is used in all sorts of contexts (head of the body, head of the school, head of the government, head of the mountain, and so forth); however, in Spanish it's impossible to say cabeza del escuela ("head of the school") – so also in Greek and in many other languages – good English is stupid Spanish. Similarly, good Greek is stupid English.

*Thus, it's one thing for native speakers to talk about "semantic domains" in terms of their own language – but it is certainly **not** a science – and many speakers (especially linguists) may disagree about many issues pertaining to them. But Louw & Nida are **not** native Greek speakers and so their pronouncements about Greek semantic domains are even more subjective and tenuous than they would be otherwise. Moreover, they have made pronouncements about New Testament Greek, not Modern Greek, and there are no native speakers available to verify whatever domains may be proposed. Therefore, proposing semantic domains for a "dead" language is mostly an exercise in futility.*

Furthermore, their lexicon is in fact based on the Greek of the New Testament, not the Greek language as a whole. It is therefore necessarily short-sighted and incomplete. James Barr wrote a wonderful book titled The Semantics of Biblical Language (SCM Press, 1961). Barr presents a devastating critique of the way that languages are abused by theologians (although he focuses on Hebrew), and in his chapter 8, he savages Kittel's Theological Dictionary. Barr's criticisms of Kittel are very good and very true, and they are equally true of Louw & Nida because they are doing the same sort of thing that Kittel did. It's most unfortunate that today's theologians are generally unaware of Barr's book.'

And as to their assertion that 'episemos' can mean 'known to', here's Professor Cervin again:

'Allow me to put a different spin on the situation: Imagine that you meet a non-native English speaker who tells you that the English word famous means "acquainted." How would you react? I would expect

that you would immediately say, "No, it doesn't." And when the non-native speaker protests, and says that his dictionary says it does, you should tell him, "Well, your dictionary is wrong." It seems to me that this is exactly what Burer and Wallace are doing with Greek.

Louw & Nida are simply wrong; not completely wrong ("outstanding, famous, notorious, infamous" are valid senses), but wrong nonetheless ("well known, clearly shown, revealed" are not valid). If 'episemos' means "revealed" then famous means "acquainted"! It's the same sort of mistake.'

Burer and Wallace's assertion, as quoted above, maintains that the lexical domain can 'roughly be broken down into two streams'. Having considered the entries in the lexicons they refer to the question has to be asked; where is the lexical evidence for these two streams? It cannot be in the first two lexicons as they don't include 'known to' as a possible meaning, which leaves the entry in Louw & Nida.

On a superficial examination it might appear that the entry in Louw & Nida supports the 'two steams' assertion. It gives different possible meanings for 'episemos'. However, on closer examination that apparent support falls away. The possible meanings are put into different numerical categories and in the first category it lists 'well known' and 'outstanding'. In the second it lists 'famous', 'notorious'. Thus, although it gives two different categories, or streams, it puts 'known to' in the same category or stream as 'outstanding'. It is not clear on what basis Burer and Wallace consider this to be evidence of two streams, particularly because they simply assert the existence of two streams in their paper without referring to or dealing with any of the actual lexical entries.

For sake of completeness let us consider the entries in one more lexicon which was not referred to by Burer and Wallace, namely Thayer's Greek-English Lexicon of the New Testament. This lexicon is certainly better known than Louw & Nida and it has an entry for 'episemos' as follows:

- *having a mark on it, marked, stamped, coined, marked*
- *in a good sense of note, illustrious*
- *in a bad sense notorious, infamous*

So, once again, we have a well known Greek lexicon, which simply does not support Burer and Wallace's assertion.

Commenting on this assertion that there are 'two streams', Professor Cervin states:

> *'As far as I can tell, Burer and Wallace's "two streams" are an "implied comparative sense" and an "elative sense," but these distinctions strike me as being thoroughly artificial; the foisting of modern English categories onto an ancient Greek word. This is a dreadful mistake, exactly the sort of thing that Barr strongly condemns. Furthermore, Burer and Wallace's wording seems to imply that the word 'episemos' in and of itself essentially entails comparison, but this is just not true. The word is used in all sorts of contexts where there is no comparison at all. 'episemos' essentially means "marked" – the notion of comparison is largely irrelevant. This is best seen in LSJ; is obscured in BAGD; is not at all evident in L&N.'*

But the alleged 'two streams' are fundamental to Burer and Wallace's argument. Without them their thesis falls apart. It is the alleged 'two streams' that allow them to adopt the categories of 'inclusive' and 'exclusive'. We know from footnote 13 in their paper that in using these terms they said they were taking their cue from Professor Cervin. It is therefore even more interesting to see what Professor Cervin has to say about this categorisation:

> *'Burer and Wallace say that their "inclusive"/"exclusive" categorization was taken from me (p. 79 of their article), but I am afraid that they have misunderstood me to begin with. In my Junia article (p. 470), I was referring to the two major interpretations of the Romans passage in question; whether Andronicus and Junia were to be understood as included among the apostles ("inclusive") or not ("exclusive"). I was not trying to establish any sort of semantic categories for the word 'episemos'. Burer and Wallace have put words in my mouth.'*

So, in short, there is no evidence for the alleged 'two streams' and they have misunderstood what Professor Cervin was saying when he was referring to 'inclusive' and 'exclusive'. It follows that the lexicons are no friend of Burer and Wallace's thesis.

Turning to syntactical evidence, it is worth reminding ourselves of Burer and Wallace's central assertion. They contend that 'en' plus the Dative is 'exclusive', and 'en' plus the Dative is not used with comparative or implied comparative personal nouns.

It is interesting to note that at no point in their paper do Burer and Wallace cite any Greek grammar in support of their assertion. This is particularly strange when one considers that they are asserting a meaning that they say was a common and standard use of the word in New Testament Greek.

As explained in the summary, Burer and Wallace are keen to ensure we compare apples with apples. However, before narrowing our examination to the criteria laid down by Burer and Wallace, it will be informative first to consider some more general examples of the word 'en' followed by a noun in the Dative to see if they shed any light on the issue of 'inclusive' v 'exclusive'.

Below are five passages taken from the ESV Bible, first in New Testament Greek and then in English. I have specifically chosen the ESV Bible as it is one of the few which has accepted Burer and Wallace's thesis and adopted it when translating Romans 16:7. Each passage contains the word 'en' which is then followed by a noun in the Dative. It can be seen that in each passage there is no doubt that an 'inclusive' meaning is conveyed. For example, in Matt 2:6 Bethlehem was 'among' the rulers of Judah, not 'known to' the rulers of Judah. In Acts 4:34 the needy people were 'among' them, not 'known to' them. And in 1 Peter 5:1 Peter exalted the elders who were 'among' them, not 'known to' them.

Matt 2:6

καὶ σύ Βηθλέεμ γῆ Ἰούδα οὐδαμῶς ἐλαχίστη εἶ ἐν

τοῖς ἡγεμόσιν Ἰούδα

And you, O Bethlehem, in the land of Judah, are by no means least among the rulers of Judah;

Acts 4:34

οὐδὲ γὰρ ἐνδεής τις ἦν ἐν αὐτοῖς

There was not a needy person among them

Acts 15:22

Ἰούδαν τὸν καλούμενον Βαρσαββᾶν καὶ Σιλᾶν

ἄνδρας ἡγουμένους ἐν τοῖς ἀδελφοῖς

Judas called Barsabbas, and Silas, leading men among the brothers

Gal 1:14

καὶ προέκοπτον ἐν τῷ Ἰουδαϊσμῷ ὑπὲρ πολλοὺς

συνηλικιώτας ἐν τῷ γένει μου

And I was advancing in Judaism beyond many of my own age among my people

1 Peter 5:1

πρεσβυτέρους οὖν ἐν ὑμῖν παρακαλῶ

So I exhort the elders among you

Commenting on these five examples Professor Cervin states:

'Linguistically, there are two issues here: (1) What does 'episemos' mean? and (2) What does 'en' plus dative mean?

The short answer to (1) is: 'episemos' means "marked; notable, remarkable, prominent; etc." (in both positive and negative senses – see LSJ).

The short answer to (2) is: 'en' plus dative means "in, within, among, in the midst of; during; etc." (with reference to place, time, manner, or state – again, see LSJ). All of the NT examples above simply confirm this.

However, Burer and Wallace are evidently taking the entire phrase "episemos en plus dative" as an idiom to mean something completely different (i.e., "known to") and in doing this they are simply mistaken. "episemos en plus dative" is not a Greek idiom. If it were an idiom, LSJ would have an entry to that effect (they are generally very good about this sort of thing).

By idiom I mean the standard linguistic notion that two or more words are combined in a unique way so as to produce a unique meaning that cannot be inferred from the component parts. For example, the English idiom hit the ceiling means "become very angry" and has nothing whatsoever to do with hitting anything nor with ceilings. My English Second Language students hate these sorts of things because they can't figure out the meanings from the parts. No one can; that's why they're called idioms (from the Greek ἴδιον meaning "one's own; particular, private, unique, distinctive"). Native speakers, however, understand idioms perfectly because they are treated and learned just like words. We don't even think about them; we just understand.

*Language is not like math. In math, 2 + 2 = 4, ever and always unto the ages of ages. Nothing will ever change that math fact. However, language is **different**. In one context, 2 + 2 = 4 (this is the "literal meaning"), but in a different context, 2 + 2 = 12.75 (this is the "idiom"); it makes sense to no one except native speakers. It looks like a duck, but it's really a parrot. Very many people simply don't understand this. They want language to be like math, but that ain't the way the language world works!*

The impression I have is that Burer and Wallace cannot read simple Greek because they can neither understand 'episemos' nor en plus dative.'

The simple fact is that these five examples (and there are many more in the New Testament) provide strong evidence against Burer and Wallace's theory. However, Burer and Wallace rule these examples as inadmissible because they are not comparing apples with apples. For one, they do not contain the word 'episemos'. Applying Burer and Wallace's rules of evidence (which have been arbitrarily determined by them) we are restricted to considering 30 passages only. The lexical and syntactical evidence so far having failed to support Burer and Wallace's case, to those 30 passages we must now turn.

Chapter 20

Biblical and Patristic Greek

Before considering specific passages it will assist to summarise the evidence cited by Burer and Wallace and the conclusions they draw from it.

In this category there is a total of 7 examples which are set out below. Five of these appear and are dealt with the in the main text and two are referred to in a footnote (no. 52). The seven passages are each categorised as being either i) 'inclusive' or 'exclusive' ii) Genitive or Dative and; iii) personal or impersonal.

Main Text
3 Macc 6.1	Inclusive – Genitive – personal
Pss. Sol 17.30	Inclusive - Genitive – impersonal
Mart. Pol 14.1	Inclusive - Genitive – impersonal
Add. Esth 16.22	Inclusive – Dative – impersonal
Pss. Sol 2.6	Exclusive – Dative – personal

Footnote
1 Macc 11.37	Inclusive – Dative - impersonal
1 Macc 14.48	Inclusive – Dative- impersonal

From these seven passages Burer and Wallace draw five conclusions. As these are based on the categorization of each passage it will assist to set out the passages that relate to each conclusion.

The first conclusion they draw is that when the word 'episemos' is being used in a comparative sense it is *'frequently if not usually in the Genitive'*. You may recall from chapter 15 that 'comparative' is the same as 'inclusive'. From the seven examples above it can be seen that six of them are 'inclusive', so the conclusion *'frequently if not usually in the Genitive'* is drawn from six examples.

Main Text
3 Macc 6.1	Inclusive – Genitive – personal
Pss. Sol 17.30	Inclusive - Genitive – impersonal
Mart. Pol 14.1	Inclusive - Genitive – impersonal
Add. Esth 16.22	Inclusive – Dative – impersonal

Footnote
1 Macc 11.37	Inclusive – Dative - impersonal
1 Macc 14.48	Inclusive – Dative- impersonal

The question has to be asked as to exactly what is meant by *'frequently if not usually'*?

If the examples from the footnote are included, then in three out of six of the examples (50%) 'episemos' is used with the Genitive when it is being used in the comparative/inclusive sense. It is surely stretching the everyday meaning of the English language to describe 50% of the time as being *'frequently if not usually'*. Plus, on Burer and Wallace's definition the exact opposite conclusion could equally be drawn, namely that *'frequently if not usually'* (three out of six examples - 50% of the time) 'episemos' is used with the Dative when it is being used in the comparative/inclusive sense.

The question must also be asked as to why the two examples which contradict Burer and Wallace's thesis are relegated to the footnote and not dealt with in the main text. One answer to that could be that they were (wrongly) not considered to fall within the category of Biblical and patristic Greek, but whilst that might remove the problem of selective citations in the main text, it simply moves the problem on, as will be seen below.

The second conclusion Burer and Wallace draw is that when 'episemos' is used in the elative/exclusive sense, *'en plus personal plural Dative is not uncommon'*

At this point I would ask you to look again at the list of seven examples above. We are now considering only those examples that fall in the 'exclusive' category. Based on the examples which fall within this category Burer and Wallace conclude that *'en plus personal plural Dative is **not uncommon** (emphasis mine)'*

Does it surprise you to see that there is only one example in this category?

> Pss. Sol 2.6   Exclusive – Dative – personal

So, having searched over 60 million Greek words, having produced results running to *'several hundred pages of text'* and having manually narrowed the results to 'a few dozen', Burer and Wallace have managed to find a total of one example in Biblical and patristic Greek where 'episemos' is used in the elative/exclusive sense and is followed by 'en plus personal plural Dative'.

The question that screams out from this is how exactly can one single example sensibly and honestly be described as being *'not uncommon'*?

Their third conclusion is that the 'inclusive' view is *'aided in some impersonal constructions'*

As with the first conclusion, we are now only considering those six examples where episemos is used in a comparative sense. Of those six, three apply to this conclusion, in that they are inclusive, Dative and impersonal.

> Main Text
> Add. Esth 16.22   Inclusive – Dative – impersonal
>
> Footnote
> 1 Macc 11.37   Inclusive – Dative - impersonal
> 1 Macc 14.48   Inclusive – Dative- impersonal

Thus, in three out of six examples, when 'episemos' is used in the inclusive sense it is followed by 'en' plus impersonal plural Dative. These three examples obviously go against Burer and Wallace's thesis and it is interesting to see how they treat examples that do not assist their case. Only one is dealt with in the main text, the other two being relegated to a footnote. And applying the same logic behind their first conclusion, we are able to conclude from three out of six examples that when 'episemos' is used in the comparative sense it is *frequently if not usually* followed by en plus the Dative.

You will recall that one possible explanation for the two examples not being dealt with in the main text is that they do not fall within the category of Biblical and patristic Greek. Even if this explanation was correct (which it isn't because the examples clearly fall within the period of Biblical and patristic Greek), it now becomes clear that it is untenable in any event. The reason for this is that the third conclusion refers to *'some impersonal constructions'*. As *'some'* cannot possibly be 'one', and as there is only one example if the two in the footnote are excluded, it must follow that Burer and Wallace accept that the two examples in the footnote fall within the category of Biblical and patristic Greek.

It is illuminating to consider how Burer and Wallace's interpretation of evidence changes depending on whether or not it supports their thesis. When 50% of the examples support their case they are described as *'frequently if not usually'*, but when 50% contradict their case the opposing view is said to be *'aided by some [examples]'*

Their fourth conclusion is that *'every instance of personal inclusiveness used a Genitive'*.

As with their second conclusion, I would ask you once again to look at the list of seven examples above. We are now considering only those examples that fall into the category of 'inclusive' and personal. Please also bear in mind that in respect of the examples which are 'inclusive' and personal Burer and Wallace conclude that *'in every instance'* the Genitive is used.

Does it surprise you to see that there is only one example in this category?

3 Macc 6.1   Inclusive – Genitive – personal

Frankly Burer and Wallace's abuse of the English language is getting beyond a joke. It is unarguable that any semi-literate English speaking person would understand the phrase *'in every instance'* to be in the plural, i.e. referring to more than one. One can only conclude that Burer and Wallace did not approach this matter in a fair minded way, but instead set out with an a priori position that Junia was not an apostle which in turn led to a selective treatment of the evidence and a willingness to present it in a misleading way.

Their fifth conclusion is as equally misleading as their fourth. They state that *'every instance'* of 'en' plus personal plural Dative was 'exclusive'.

As we now have some idea as to what Burer and Wallace mean by *'every instance'*, it won't surprise you to learn that once again we are talking about one example. Of the seven listed above, only one has 'en' followed by personal plural in the Dative.

Pss. Sol 2.6 – Exclusive – Dative – personal

If there is a crumb of comfort in this egregious abuse of the English language I suppose it is that they are least consistent.

Putting the evidence for all five conclusions together, and particularly the fifth, it can be seen that there is in fact only one example in the whole of Biblical and patristic Greek which supports Burer and Wallace's thesis. They set out to prove that whenever 'episemos' is used in an 'exclusive' sense it will be followed by 'en' plus the personal plural Dative, and managed to uncover only one example where this occurs.

It might be said that we need go no further in our examination of the evidence from Biblical and patristic Greek. Certainly a single example would appear to be an entirely insufficient evidential foundation on which to base a theory, but notwithstanding this fact it beholds us to examine the evidence to see if even this single example really does support their case.

The sole example from Biblical and patristic Greek that is said to support their thesis is Pss. Sol 2.6 (exclusive – Dative – personal). In respect of this passage they state:

> *This construction comes as close to Rom 16:7 as any we have yet seen. The parallels include (a) people as the referent of the adjective [episemos], (b) followed by [en] plus the dative plural, (c) the dative plural referring to people as well. All the key elements are here.*

At this point it is also worth remembering that according to footnote 45, although Burer and Wallace refer to this example, the actual translation of it was apparently done by Chris Bradley.

So, here's the passage as it appears in the paper

ἐπισήμῳ ἐν τοῖς ἔθνεσιν

And here it is in its actual context

οἱ υἱοὶ καὶ αἱ θυγατέρες ἐν αἰχμαλωσίᾳ πονηρᾷ, ἐν σφραγῖδι ὁ τράχηλος αὐτῶν, ἐν ἐπισήμῳ ἐν τοῖς ἔθνεσιν

If you compare these two texts you will see that the one from the paper starts with the word 'ἐπισήμῳ', whereas when the full text is looked at the word 'ἐπισήμω' appears half way through the sentence. In particular, and of crucial importance, the word 'ἐπισήμω' follows on immediately from the word 'en' (ἐν) and is in fact sandwiched between two of them. Burer and Wallace have concentrated on the second of the two 'en's', but without getting too technical, it is beyond doubt from a New Testament Greek point of view that the first 'en' relates to the word 'ἐπισήμω' which immediately follows it. It is therefore surprising, putting it mildly, that Burer and Wallace start their quotation from this passage with the word 'ἐπισήμω' and leave out the first 'en'.

But Burer and Wallace's real error is even more basic and inexcusable. As you know, Burer and Wallace have been comparing the **adjective** 'episemos' and they have been very keen to insist on comparing apples with apples. It is therefore somewhat surprising to see that in this example the word 'ἐπισήμω' is not in fact an adjective. The word 'ἐπισήμω' is in fact 'episemon', which is a **noun**. This causes serious problems for Burer and Wallace, because if 'episemon' is not an adjective, the passage in question is no longer a close parallel to Romans 16:7. Absent this example, which must now surely be ignored, Burer and Wallace are left without a single example from Biblical and patristic Greek that supports their theory. And if you think I'm splitting hairs about 'episemon' not being an adjective, remember that Burer and Wallace discount examples just because the noun is impersonal as opposed to personal.

But you don't have to take my word for it. Professor Cervin's comments will leave you in do doubt.

> *'Here, Burer and Wallace are simply wrong, and their error is ironically made explicit in the translation of this Psalm of Solomon which they themselves print in their article:* *"they were **a spectacle** among the gentiles."* *The word used in Ps. Sol. 2:6 is **not** the adjective 'episemos' but the noun 'episemon'. It's just simple Greek grammar. So, Ps. Sol. 2:6 is "parallel"*

*to Rom. 16:7, containing "all the key elements"??
Rubbish!!*

*As a general comment to all of the preceding: I think
that Burer and Wallace's three-fold categorization
(in(ex)clusive – genitive/dative – (im)personal) is
rather absurd. It appears that they are taking a
disputed interpretation of Rom. 16:7 – taking their cue
from me (so they say), whom they've simply
misunderstood to begin with! – and turning that
disputed interpretation into a litmus test which they
then foist onto other Greek texts and contexts, most of
which are nothing at all like Rom. 16:7. The only
words I can think of to describe this "method" is
ludicrous, absurd, idiotic. (I'm trying to be polite.)
Also, it seems to me that half the time they don't even
understand the Greek grammar involved – either
another preposition is used (e.g., ἐχ) which forces the
use of the genitive case, or there are other semantic
reasons for the uses of the cases other than their so-
called "inclusive/exclusive" ideas (e.g., partitive).
Their whole scheme is just rubbish.'*

Conclusion

Burer and Wallace's treatment of the evidence is simply
untenable. Their use of language is, to put it mildly, misleading,
and the evidence does not support their conclusions. The simple
fact is that they have been unable to produce a single example
from Biblical and patristic Greek that supports their theory. On the
contrary, what examples they have produced clearly demonstrate
that when 'episemos' is followed by 'en' plus the Dative it has an
inclusive/comparative meaning.

And things don't get any better for Burer and Wallace when we
look at the evidence from papyri.

Chapter 21

Papyri

In respect of the Papyri Burer and Wallace state

> *The papyri can be dispensed with relatively quickly, as there are only a few examples of [episemos] in them*

As you will see from page 12/87 of the paper, the section on papyri takes up only one paragraph and Burer and Wallace were unable to find a single example from the papyri which supported their theory, i.e. there was not a single example of 'en' plus the Dative carrying an 'exclusive' meaning.

The length of this chapter is directly proportionate to the strength of their case – at least in respect of the papyri.

Chapter 22

Inscriptions and Literary texts

<u>Inscriptions</u>

In the evidential category of inscriptions Burer and Wallace are able to muster up four examples.

1 Tam 2.905.1 west wall. Coll. 2.5.18

Tam 2.1-3.838

Tam 2.1-3.905 west wall. Coll 3.12

Fd Xanth 7.76.1.1.1.1.4

In respect of all four examples they assert that they are 'exclusive', have 'en' plus the Dative, are excellent parallels and point in one direction. They go on to state that like Biblical and patristic Greek, they supply a uniform picture of 'episemos' with personal nouns. As we have seen, that last statement about Biblical and patristic Greek is at odds with what the evidence actually shows, and as we are about to see, so are their statements about the inscriptions.

Although four examples are claimed in support of their theory, only one is actually quoted and discussed in the main text. *1 Tam 2.905. west wall.coll.2.5.18.*

Here it is in the Greek

οὐ μόνον ἐ]ν τῇ [π]ατρίδι πρώτου, ἀλλὰ [καὶ ἐν τῷ ἔθ]νει ἐπισήμου.

134

And here is the translation that appears in the paper (by Chris Bradley?)

> 'Not only foremost in his own country, but also well known to the outside population'

Clearly this translation amounts to an 'exclusive' example. The person being referred to is not part of the outside population (inclusive) he is outside of it (exclusive).

To quote from the paper, Burer and Wallace say of this example:

> 'Here the person who is ἐπισῆμου is called such only in relation to outsiders (πρῶτου is used in relation to his own countrymen). It is not insignificant that **en** plus the dative personal noun is used: the man is well known to a group of which he is not a member'

And at footnote 53 they say

> 'ἔθνει here evidently refers to outsiders—that is, a group to which this man does not belong. This is evident from the strong contrast between the two phrases (οὐ μόνον. . . ἀλλὰ καὶ,), with the man's fame receiving the laudatory note with the ascensive καὶ, hinting that such a commendation is coming.'

The problem with this example is that not only are Burer and Wallace using their own translation, but they are also using their own definitions of Greek words. This can be demonstrated if we translate the text using Greek lexicons, i.e. if we only use words that appear in lexicons as being possible meanings for the Greek words. Here's a literal translation

> *'Not only first in his own part of the country (in his own native city), but also outstanding and eminent in the nation.'*

In short, this example is only exclusive if the Greek word 'ethnos' (εθνος or εθνει) means the 'outside population'. Let's look at an extract from the entry in Liddell Scott Jones for the word 'ethnos'

> *'ἔθνος, εος, τό: -number of people living together, company, body of men, band of comrades,.; ἔθνος λαῶν host of men, of particular tribes, of animals, ἔ. μελισσάων, ὀρνίθων, μυιάων, swarms, flocks, etc.,*
> *2. after Hom., nation, people, b. later, τὰ ἔ. foreign, barbarous nations, opp; at Athens, athletic clubs of non-Athenians, non-Jews, Gentiles, used of Gentile Christians*
> *3. class of men, caste, tribe, the orders of priests, trade-associations or guilds*
> *II. of a single person, a relation.'*

If we use the most obvious and prominent meaning from the possibilities listed in LSJ in our translation, then what Burer and Wallace translated as 'the outside population' becomes 'in the nation', which in turn means that the example switches from being allegedly 'exclusive' to clearly 'inclusive'. In order for Burer and Wallace's translation to be correct we would have to adopt a meaning which LSJ describes as being, *'b. later, τὰ ἔ. foreign, barbarous nations.* Such a meaning simply does not fit with the context of the passage. Thus, the only one of the four examples that is actually dealt with in the text turns out to be the opposite of what they say it is.

It is interesting to note that they only quote one example. They say that all four support their case, but only deal with one. Human nature being what it is, it is safe to assume that the one they dealt with was the one they considered to be the most supportive of the four examples. But that same human nature compels me to examine at least one of the remaining three examples that they don't deal with.

The fourth example is *Fd Xanth 7.76.1.1.1.1.4*. Here it is in the Greek:

προγόνω[ν Λυκιαρχη]σάντων καὶ στρ[ατηγη]σάντων
καὶ να[αρχησαν] των τοῦ ἔθν[ους καὶ] ἐν ταῖς ὑπερ
Ῥωμ[αὶων] συμμαχίαις ἐπί[σημον?] γενόμενον,
γ[ραμματεύ]σαντα τοῦ Λυκί[ων εθνους] λαμπρῶς καὶ
μ[εγαλοψύ]χως

And here's the translation:

'president of the Lycians, general and admiral of the nation, prominent among Rome's allies, secretary of the Lycian nation, illustrious and great.'

I simply cannot comprehend how Burer and Wallace can think this example is 'exclusive'. The whole point of the text is the fact that the president of the Lycians was an ally of Rome. The text would become completely meaningless if he was not an ally of Rome. He was not 'known to' Rome's allies, he was counted 'among' Rome's allies. This is a very close parallel to Romans 16:7, it has an 'inclusive' meaning and yet it is not dealt with in the main text. This is a serious failing on behalf of Burer and Wallace and one that does them no credit at all.

I will spend no more time on the Inscriptions. They simply do not support Burer and Wallace's thesis.

Literary Texts

Here they state that the evidence is not so uniform. You will forgive me for asking; as uniform as what? But they go on state that the *'pattern that has emerged is still generally maintained.'* Again, exactly what pattern would that be?

Three examples are given, which means that Burer and Wallace believe a pattern can emerge from only three examples. The three examples are:

> *Lycurgus, Against Leocrates 129*
> *Euripides Bacch 967*
> *Euripides Hipp 103*

Would it surprise you to learn that in the first two examples, the word 'en' does not appear? That's right, the same Burer and Wallace who insist on comparing apples with apples, who discount examples if the nouns are impersonal as opposed to personal, are here putting forward examples in support of their thesis which do not contain one of the very words in dispute! Remember, their thesis is that passages where 'episemos' is followed by 'en' plus the personal plural Dative have an 'exclusive' meaning. And yet they apparently think it is acceptable to cite passages in support of their thesis that don't even contain the word 'en'.

That leaves one remaining example. And at first blush it appears that finally, for the very first time, Burer and Wallace have found an example that supports their theory. The word 'en' is present, it is followed by the Dative and the meaning appears to be clearly 'exclusive'. Indeed, some other critics of Burer and Wallace have been prepared to accept this example as a valid instance of 'en' plus Dative being 'exclusive' and therefore supporting their theory. I am not inclined to be so charitable.

As I see it there are two objections to this example being prayed in aid of Burer and Wallace's case. The first and less significant of the two is that this example dates to a period 500 years before Paul wrote Romans and everyone accepts there is a significant difference between the Greek of that era and the Greek of the New Testament. In particular, the meaning of the word 'episemos' changed during the period of time which separates this example from Romans 16:7.

The second objection is more fundamental. Put simply, Burer and Wallace make the mistake of asserting that 1 plus 1 equals 3. If one considers their argument carefully, it can be seen that it involves drawing a conclusion from two separate facts.

Facts
i) this passage has 'en' plus the Dative;
ii) the meaning is 'exclusive'

Conclusion
'en' plus the Dative (must/should/normally/usually) carry an exclusive meaning

It simply does not follow as a matter of logic that these two facts justify the conclusion. This becomes clear when you consider Professor Cervin's comments on this example and the conclusion Burer and Wallace seek to draw from it.

> 'Euripides' play opens with Aphrodite plotting the death of Hippolytus because the latter worships Artemis and pays scant attention to Aphrodite ("hell hath no fury like a goddess scorned"!) – there's a back-story to this situation, which isn't relevant to Burer and Wallace's article. Anyway, in the play, after Aphrodite's opening statement, Hippolytus and some of his servants enter, and one of these servants gently chides Hippolytus regarding his disdain for Aphrodite. During this exchange with Hippolytus, the servant says, referring to Aphrodite:
>
> σεμνή γε μέντοι χἀπίσημος ἐν βροτοῖς. (line 103)
>
> "[she is] august indeed and moreover [is] notable (or remarkable) among mortals"

Obviously, Aphrodite is not a mortal so she cannot be reckoned among the category of mortals; i.e., she is "excluded" from the group of mortals as Burer and Wallace would categorize the verse, appealing to the grammar 'en' plus Dative. Now, according to Burer and Wallace's ill-logic, because the same grammar ('en' plus Dative) is used in Rom. 16:7 regarding Andronicus and Junia, therefore they also must be reckoned as "excluded" from the category of apostles.

However, as I read and thought about Euripides' text, it occurred to me to put a twist on the verse in question. Suppose I were to say of St. Paul, for example, that he is:

σεμνός γε μέντοι χἀπίσημος ἐν βροτοῖς.

*Would this therefore mean that St. Paul must be excluded from the category of mortals? Burer and Wallace must agree because Greek grammar says so ('en' plus Dative)! Obviously, this would be a foolish and utterly false conclusion, for St. Paul **is** a mortal. But Euripides' verse here could well be said of any number of characters, either gods or mortals. To look at this verse from yet another angle, one could ask, "What do mortals think of Aphrodite?" And the answer, in Euripides' words, would be, "They think she's august and remarkable." Now, what about St. Paul? What do mortals think of him? Similarly, "They think he's august and remarkable." There is nothing at all unusual about this in terms of Greek grammar.*

The problem (as I mentioned in my comments to you earlier) is that Burer and Wallace simply can't read Greek beyond the NT (and therefore they misunderstand the NT). They naively assume that the question of whether Andronicus and Junia are to be reckoned as being within the category of the apostles (their "inclusive") or not (their "exclusive") is determined by the grammar of 'en' plus Dative. However, this entire question really has nothing whatsoever to do with Greek grammar! 'en' plus Dative has nothing to do with it!

Looking again at how Burer and Wallace briefly explained this verse in Hippolytus (on their p.88), and then considering the entire text in context, it struck me anew how ignorant and misguided Burer and Wallace are, both in their understanding of Greek grammar and in terms of their linguistic "analysis".'

Accordingly, Burer and Wallace's thesis finds no support from any of the examples they cite from literary texts. As it happens, I entirely agree with their statement concerning literary texts when they say that the *'pattern that has emerged is still generally maintained.'* It's just that I'm seeing an entirely different *'pattern'* to the one they had in mind.

Chapter 23

Hellenistic

In respect of examples from Hellenistic Greek, Burer and Wallace say they are a *'bit more varied in nuances'* and that *'impersonal examples go both ways'*.

Dealing first with impersonal examples, three are cited in the paper:

> *Lucianus, De Meretri 1.2*
> *Rufus Medicus*
> *Philo Fug.10*

Burer and Wallace accept that these three are all 'en' followed by the Dative and are 'inclusive'. In other words, all three go against their thesis, but of course Burer and Wallace discount them because they contain impersonal as opposed to personal nouns.

A fourth example is then cited as being 'inclusive' but in the Genitive, not the Dative

> *Galen De Methodo Medendi*

A couple of observations need to be made. First, when Burer and Wallace said the impersonal examples *'go both ways'* what they actually meant is that 75% of them go one way and 25% go the other way. Secondly, that all of them were 'inclusive'. This last point is worth considering in more detail. What the examples show is that 'episemos' can have an 'inclusive' meaning when either the Genitive or the Dative is used. But that is uncontroversial. No one is saying that in order for 'episemos' to have an inclusive meaning it MUST be followed by the Dative. The controversy is over whether it can or does have an 'inclusive' meaning when it is followed by the Dative. Burer and Wallace contend that it does not, but unfortunately for them their contention is void of any supporting evidence.

At this point Burer and Wallace turn to the personal examples, which of course they consider to be much more relevant to their thesis. They also return to their old habit of stretching the normal meaning of English words, as they state that there are 'several' personal examples, when in fact there are only three.

Here are the first two examples

Lucianus – Harmonides – the pipe player

Lucianus Peregr 6.1 - famous ones among men of old

On the face of it the first one supports their thesis. It is 'en' followed by the personal Dative and it is exclusive. The second one also supports their thesis in that it is in the Genitive and is inclusive. However, it is impossible to know whether what they say about the second example is correct because, as Professor Cervin points out:

> *'This reference is wrong. Peregr. is the abbreviation for De Morte Peregrini ("On the Death of Peregrinus") and the Greek phrase that Burer and Wallace cite on their p. 89 does not in fact occur here at all; nor does the phrase occur in sections 1 thru 8 of De Morte Peregrini'*

Buoyed by this apparent evidence in support of their thesis Burer and Wallace declare, after only two examples (one of which doesn't exist), that they show the *'same patterns we saw earlier'*.

The third example is *Lucianus – On Salaried Posts in Great Houses.* This example contains 'en' followed by the personal Dative and in respect of it Burer and Wallace state

> *'It is unmistakable, it is personal it is rare.'*

In other words, this example is the exact opposite of what their thesis says. It is 'inclusive'.

However, not for the first time, Burer and Wallace appear to be having some problems with their citations, a fact again pointed out by Professor Cervin

> 'It certainly is rare because, again, the reference is
> WRONG. In their footnote 64, they identify this work
> as Merc. Cond. 2.8 which is De Mercede conductis.
> The English translation On Salaried Posts in Great
> Houses is correct, but it is also known as The
> Dependent Scholar. I have Lucian's text in front of me
> and this sentence does NOT occur in section 2.8
> (again, ".8" is meaningless); it actually occurs in
> section 28. In context, the phrase here is obviously
> "inclusive" (Burer and Wallace don't flatly deny this)
> because the individual referred to is in the midst of
> (en) a musical procession. However, their comment
> "It is unmistakable, it is personal, and it is rare" is
> simply false.'

So, on Burer and Wallace's own case there are two examples of 'en' followed by the personal Dative, of which one supports their thesis and the other does not. One is 'inclusive', one is 'exclusive'. But that's before we look more closely at the one they say supports their thesis.

> *Lucianus – Harmonides – the pipe player*

Burer and Wallace's translation of this example reads

> *Glory before the crowds, fame among the masses*

However, a more accurate translation is

> *To be distinguished among the multitude*
> *To be the conspicuous one in a crowd*

Put simply, the context of this passage demands an 'inclusive' meaning as opposed to the 'exclusive' meaning, which Burer and

Wallace seek. The pipe player wanted to stand out from the crowd. He was in that crowd and he wanted to stand out, he wanted to be the conspicuous one in the crowd. Thus, the pipe player was a member of, was in the crowd. He was 'included' in the crowd. He was not outside the crowd; he was in it and wanted to stand out. As it is referring to someone who was a member of the crowd, this example is 'inclusive'.

This 'inclusive' interpretation is supported by Professor Cervin

> *'They rightly say that the further context of this passage indicates that Harmonides wants to be singled out by the crowd – "to be pointed at" – and this implies that Harmonides is right there in the midst of the crowd, which is exactly what the phrase means to begin with! One cannot "point out" someone who is absent. In fact, a bit later in §1, Harmonides tells Timotheus, his teacher, that he (Harm.) wants to be just like Tim. and have everyone fawn all over him whenever he walks into a room. Again, this necessarily implies that Harmonides would be in the midst of the crowd. It is much more likely that this passage is in fact "inclusive" and thus is contradictory to Burer and Wallace's thesis'*

Accordingly, neither of the 'en' plus personal Dative examples supports their thesis.

Burer and Wallace then deal very briefly with two other examples. The first, *Jos. Bell 2.418,* is referred to in the main text and is said to support the 'inclusive' view. It is not discussed in any detail (it does not support their thesis) and it is said to be *'not a clean parallel.'*

The second example is not dealt with in the main text but instead appears at footnote 65 where it is stated as being *Lucianus Peregr 22.2*

Unfortunately Burer and Wallace's use of incorrect citations is becoming a bit of a habit, because once again this reference simply does not exist. However, after much searching it appears the example they meant to cite was in fact *Lucian. Dialogues of the Dead 22(27).2.*

Here it is in the Greek

Καὶ ἄλλοι μὲν πολλοὶ συγκατέβαινον ἡμῖν, ἐν αὐτοῖς

δὲ ἐπίσημοι Ἰσμηνόδωπός τε ὁ πλούσιος ὁ ἡμέτερος καὶ

Ἀρσάκης ὁ Μηδίας ὕπαρχος καὶ Ὀροίτης ὁ Ἀρμένιος

And here's the translation

We had quite a crowd with us on our way down; most distinguished among whom were our rich countryman Ismenodorus ...

The rich countryman was part of the crowd; he was 'among' the crowd. This example is 'en' plus the personal Dative and it is 'inclusive.' Which means that this example, which was relegated to a footnote, not discussed at all and given an incorrect reference, points in the opposite direction to that contended for by Burer and Wallace.

You may well be wondering how it is possible that Burer and Wallace were able to provide so many incorrect citations in their paper. You may also be wondering how the editors of New Testament Studies did not pick up these incorrect citations before the paper was published. The following explanation from Professor Cervin goes some way to explaining.

'In the field of Classics there are standard ways of referring to authors and texts, just as there are standard chapter and verse references for the Bible. What would you think if you read someone who quoted, "For God so loved the world that He gave his only-

begotten Son ..." and gave the reference as Ioh. 1427? With the name abbreviated incorrectly and a page number instead of chapter and verse, you should be rather confused. And if you had to suffer a number of such bungles, I expect that you would get rather irritated trying to find the correct references. Greek and Latin texts have standardized numbering so that anyone can find any passage regardless of the edition that anyone is using (just like the Bible). Further, any good English translation of Greek or Latin literature will also provide the standard numeration in the margin, or somewhere, for ease of reference to the original text. Burer and Wallace's not using the standard references is analogous to a biologist who knows nothing about theology and who misquotes the Bible and refers to page numbers instead of the standard chapters and verses.

Standard Classical Greek and Latin texts are found in the Oxford Classical Texts series (OCT) and in the Teubner series (a German publication). Cambridge University Press also publishes a number of critical Greek and Latin editions of particular works. The Loeb Series (LCL), published by Harvard University Press, is often useful, but it is not considered "standard" by Classics scholars. Typically, a classicist would use a Loeb edition only if there were no other critical edition available. I have a bookshelf full of Oxford, Teubner, and Cambridge editions, as well as Loeb editions of Greek authors that are not readily available otherwise, and sometimes the Loeb numbering is erroneous; sometimes the Loeb text itself is erroneous. Also, just as the books of the Bible have standard abbreviations, so do Greek and Latin authors and their various works (all in Latin – it's a Classics tradition). These standard abbreviations are listed at the beginning of LSJ under the heading "Authors and Works" (LSJ, pp. xvi-xlv, plus the Supplement), so there's really no excuse for not getting them right. The problem with the theologians is that they simply do not know how to correctly cite Greek literature. They are "fish out of water." They don't know what they are doing, so they produce all sorts of nonsense (e.g., Ioh. 1427!). And of course, the editors at New Testament Studies don't know how to check the references either – or they just don't bother, which is even worse!

In their footnote 63, they refer to "Lucianus, Peregr. 6.1. This is De Morte Peregrini, but the word 'episemos' does not occur here at all. The number 6 refers to a section of Lucian's text, but the number ".1" is meaningless. I've read sections 1-8 of De Morte Peregrini in the Oxford Classical Text, and the word 'episemos' does not occur at all. Do Burer and Wallace have the wrong number? The wrong abbreviation? Nothing else in Lucian's entire corpus looks remotely like Peregr. Perhaps they have the wrong author? I have no idea.

Also in their footnote 63, they refer to a certain Herodian 1.7: Who is this supposed to be? Herodianus the Grammarian, Herodianus the Historian, or Herodianus the Rhetor? All three are listed in LSJ. Or is it someone else? Do they mean the short work called Herodotus, written by Lucian? If they do, then they have the wrong name. And what is "1.7" supposed to mean? Actually, on a lark, I looked at Lucian's Herodotus and in section 1 (vol. III, p. 346, line 10 in the OCT), the word 'episemos' does indeed occur, but contrary to Burer and Wallace, there is no genitive, nor dative, nor preposition 'en' used in that context! The number ".7" is still meaningless. There is no way to verify this reference.

I have no idea what texts Burer and Wallace were using, or if they were just pulling citations from a TLG printout. (By the way, when I was using the TLG as a graduate student at UIUC, often the numeration was erroneous. I was forever checking the printouts against published Greek texts to make sure that I had the correct references!) They refer to some Loeb editions, but the Loebs are NOT standard Greek texts – the Oxford, Teubner, or Cambridge ones are – and I know for a fact that the Loeb numbering is sometimes flat out wrong. Using non-standard texts with erroneous numbering is a recipe for disaster. But, again, Burer and Wallace are not Classicists – they don't know how to deal with Greek texts outside of the NT.'

When I discovered these incorrect references it reminded me of a paper I had read many years ago and which after much rummaging around I was able to locate. Towards the end of that paper there was a section entitled *'note on accuracy in academic work in Biblical scholarship'*. The author of that paper was critiquing another paper, the conclusions of which he disagreed with. In this particular section he did not hold back when expressing his views, as the following extract shows:

'The article is peppered with references to extra-Biblical literature and therefore gives the appearance of careful scholarship. But only someone with access to a major research library, the ability to translate extensive passages from untranslated ancient Greek literature, and many days free for such research, could ever have discovered that this is not careful scholarship. In fact, in several sections its disregard of facts is so egregious that it fails even to meet fundamental requirements of truthfulness.'

He went on to say

'People who read reference books have a right to expect that they will be basically trustworthy, and that

where evidence is cited it will, if checked, provide clear support for the points being claimed. When one does check the evidence in an article and it turns out to be unreliable or used in tendentious ways, or even non-existent, it undermines confidence in the trustworthiness of the author and in the editors and the publisher who have produced the work. Because this topic has been so controversial, one would expect that those responsible for the volume would have taken particular care to insure accuracy. But did anyone check any of this evidence? Did any editor...?'

And he didn't stop there

'The scholarly task is an exciting one, especially in the area of Biblical studies............even when we disagree with the conclusions of an article, we should be able to expect that the citations of evidence are fundamentally reliable. But the lack of care in the use of evidence as manifested in this article, if followed by others, would throw the entire scholarly process into significant decline. We would begin to wonder if we could trust anything that was claimed by anyone else unless we checked the original data for ourselves............

We may differ for our whole lives on the interpretation of facts, for that is the nature of the scholarly task. But if our citations of the facts themselves cannot be trusted, then the foundations are destroyed.'

You may be wondering what this man's views have to do with the subject at hand. Well, those are the views of a certain Professor Wayne Grudem, the senior editor of the ESV Bible and the man who was responsible for accepting the paper by Burer and Wallace as the only basis for translating Romans 16:7 in the ESV Bible with an 'exclusive' meaning. Whatever one might think of the attitude and spirit he displayed by publishing such forthright criticism of a fellow Christian scholar (although I doubt he would accept the nomenclature of 'scholar' for the person in question) there can be no doubt that what is sauce for the goose is sauce for the gander.

As has been demonstrated, it is beyond dispute that the Burer and Wallace paper contains citations which are non-existent. I would venture to suggest I have also demonstrated that their paper is far from being *'basically trustworthy'* and the examples cited do not *'provide clear support for the points being claimed.'* As Grudem said, when one discovers that the evidence in an article is *'unreliable, or used in tendentious ways, or even is non-existent,'* it undermines confidence not only in the trustworthiness of the authors (Burer and Wallace) but also *'in the editors and the publisher who have produced the work'*

Grudem was critiquing a paper on the role of women (Wayne Grudem, "The Meaning Of kephale ("Head"): An Evaluation Of New Evidence, Real And Alleged," *Journal of the Evangelical Theological Society* 44:1 (March 2001) p. 25-65). He considered that because that subject was so controversial *'one would expect that those responsible for the volume would have taken particular care to ensure accuracy'*. And he asks the rhetorical questions *'did anyone check any of this evidence? Did any editor ......?'*

As important a topic as that paper may have been covering, I think all will agree that it was not nearly as important as the task of accurately translating the Word of God. But as editor of the ESV, when he accepted this paper by Burer and Wallace, when he produced a Bible which denies Junia's apostleship, when he failed even to include a footnote to indicate a possible alternative reading, did Grudem actually check any of this evidence? Did any editor at the ESV check it?

I might disagree with Grudem on the meaning of some Greek words, but I think he and I agree on the meaning of 'hypocrite' and 'incompetent'.

Conclusion

We have checked all the evidence; we have weighed it in the balance and it has been found wanting. At the conclusion of their paper Burer and Wallace state

> 'our examination.........has revealed some surprising results'

So has ours. They go on to state:

> 'Repeatedly in biblical Greek, patristic Greek, papyri, inscriptions, classical and Hellenistic texts, our working hypothesis was borne out.'

On the contrary, on examination their working hypothesis fell apart. And yet, apparently with straight faces, they conclude their paper with the quite breath-taking assertion that:

> 'επισημοι εν τοισ αποστολοις' (episemoi en tois apostolos) <u>almost certainly</u> means "well known to the apostles"'

I think that assertion is best summed up by Professor Cervin:

> 'This claim is pure overblown rubbish of the worst sort! Of the hundreds of Ancient Greek authors and thousands of literary works extant, Burer and Wallace can only cite **two** authors from the Classical period, **five** from the post-Classical period, and **one** from the (early) Patristic period! And many of their particular examples are misunderstood, mistranslated, misquoted, not provided, or non-existent!'

Chapter 24

Conclusion

I have to say I've grown rather fond of Romans 16:7. I suspect it's one of those verses people skip over when they're reading the Bible, its significance not being immediately apparent. Part of the reason for that probably lies in the fact that it is not obvious to most English speaking readers that Junia is a woman's name. If she had been called Mary instead of Junia the significance of the verse may not have been missed. But her name wasn't Mary, it was Junia, and of that there can be no doubt.

Having considered matters in some detail, the final conclusion is actually quite straightforward and simple. As we saw in chapters 5 to 11, the arguments that seek to deny this are without merit. In fact, the evidence is so overwhelming in support of Junia being a woman that very few people continue to maintain any other position. Instead they raise questions about the meaning of the word 'apostolos'.

Those questions were addressed in chapter 12. Some still maintain that 'apostolos' means messenger. The ESV Bible includes a footnote which suggests it as a possible alternative meaning. I would venture to suggest, however, that after weighing the evidence, most if not all objective readers will conclude that 'apostolos' in Romans 16:7 was referring to apostles.

That leaves the final question; was Junia 'among' or 'known to' the apostles?

It is clear that at the time of writing, the main focus of the argument about Junia's apostolic status centres on this question. Those who deny Junia was an apostle have in the main conceded that she was a woman and that the verse is talking about apostles. However, unable to cope with having to face the inevitable consequences which would follow from accepting that there was a woman apostle, they continue to hold firm to the view that *'episemoi en tois apostolos'* means 'well known to the apostles'.

Never mind what the evidence shows, their view on women in the Church will not be shaken and they cannot allow a feminine foot in the door.

Unfortunately, inexcusably and shamefully, certain Bible translators have provided succour to those who hold this view by adopting the translation 'known to' in Romans 16:7 and citing a paper by Burer and Wallace as justification for their position.

As this is where the current argument lies and, more importantly, because we are talking about erroneous, biased and incompetent handling of the Word of God, this final question and more particularly the paper by Burer and Wallace has been considered in some detail in chapters 13 to 23. The evidence and examination speak for themselves. The question has been answered most emphatically. Junia was among the apostles.

As a final point I should clarify that this book does not purport to amount to an exhaustive treatment of the subject. There are, no doubt, other arguments which people may put forward against Junia being an apostle that I have not dealt with. However, most if not all of these do not relate to the text in Romans 16:7. As pointed out in chapter 3, some will argue against Junia being an apostle because of their interpretation of 1 Timothy 2:12. That argument is beyond the scope of this book. Other arguments have not been dealt with because time and space did not allow and because they do not deserve to be treated seriously. For example, I have heard it said that because Jesus did not appoint any women as disciples it follows that you cannot have a woman apostle. For some strange reason I have never heard those same people go on to say that because Jesus did not appoint any black men as disciples, they can't be apostles either!

As I said in chapter 3, the fact that there was a woman apostle is not determinative of all the other questions that arise in respect of the role of women in the Church. Those questions remain to be answered, but there is one question that does not.

Was there a woman apostle?

Yes. Her name was Junia. How do I know?

Because the Bible tells me so.

INDEX

Bibliography

Bauckham, Richard — *Gospel Women: Studies of the Named Women in the Gospels.* Grand Rapids: Eerdmans, 2002

Belleville, Linda — *A Re-examination of Romans 16.7 in Light of Primary Source Materials* New Test. Stud. Vol. 51, 2005, pp. 231-249

Brooten, Bernadette — *Junia: Outstanding among the Apostles (Romans 16:7).* Pp. 41-144 in *Women Priests: A Catholic Commentary on the Vatican Declaration.* Edited by Leonard and Arlene Swidler. New York: Paulist, 1977

Burer, Michael H & Wallace, Daniel B — *Was Junia Really an Apostle? A Re-examination of Rom 16:7* New Test. Stud. Vol 47, 2001, pp. 76-91

Cervin, Richard — *A Note Regarding The Name JUNIA(S) In Romans 16:7* New Test. Stud. vol. 40, 1994, pp. 464-470

Epp, Eldon J — *Junia. The First Woman Apostle* Minneapolis: Fortress, 2005

Fitzmyer, J A — *Romans.* AB 33. New York: Doubleday, 1993

Grudem, Wayne — *Evangelical Feminism and Biblical Truth: An Analysis of More Than One Hundred Disputed Questions.* Sisters, Ore.: Multnomah, 2004

McCarthy, Suzanne   *Better Bibles blog on Junia*

Payne, Philip B   *Man and Woman, One in Christ. An Exegetical and Theological Study of Paul's Letters*. Zondervan, Grand Rapids, 2009

Piper, John &
Grudem, Wayne
Editors   *Recovering Biblical Manhood and Womanhood: A Response to Evangelical Feminism*. Wheaton, Illinois: Crossway, 1991

Swanson, KJ   *The Woman Buried Under the Words: The Story of the First Female Apostle and How She Was Erased From Scripture* Summer 2008 BTI 540 Textual Synthesis: The Epistle to the Romans Dr. Jo-Ann Badley Mars Hill Graduate School

Thorley, John   *Junia, a Woman Apostle* NovT 38 (1996): 18-29

Made in the USA
Charleston, SC
01 April 2014